SAVING AMERICA FROM ITSELF
AMERICAN REVIVAL OPPORTUNITIES

How financial greed, selfishness, consumer addiction and lack of regulation caused the near collapse of America's financial markets, loss of productivity, and huge national debts which ultimately caused America's economy into depression and forced the rest of the world's economies to fall as well.

ERNST G. FRANKEL

authorHOUSE®

AuthorHouse™
1663 Liberty Drive
Bloomington, IN 47403
www.authorhouse.com
Phone: 1-800-839-8640

© 2011 Ernst G. Frankel. All rights reserved.

No part of this book may be reproduced, stored in a retrieval system, or transmitted by any means without the written permission of the author.

First published by AuthorHouse 7/14/2011

ISBN: 978-1-4634-0810-7 (dj)
ISBN: 978-1-4634-0811-4 (sc)
ISBN: 978-1-4634-0812-1 (e)

Library of Congress Control Number: 2011908343

Printed in the United States of America

Any people depicted in stock imagery provided by Thinkstock are models, and such images are being used for illustrative purposes only. Certain stock imagery © Thinkstock.

This book is printed on acid-free paper.

Because of the dynamic nature of the Internet, any web addresses or links contained in this book may have changed since publication and may no longer be valid. The views expressed in this work are solely those of the author and do not necessarily reflect the views of the publisher, and the publisher hereby disclaims any responsibility for them.

OTHER BOOKS BY ERNST G. FRANKEL

Ocean Transportation, 1974
Management and Operations of American Shipping, 1982
Regulation and Policies of American Shipping, 1982
Port Planning and Development, 1987
The World Shipping Industry, 1987
Systems Reliability and Risk Analysis, 1988
Pursuit of Technological Excellence, 1993
Project Management in Engineering Services and Development, 1995
Ocean Environmental Management, 1995
American Institutional Dilemma, 1998
Managing Development, 2005
Challenging American Leadership, 2006
Oil and Security, 2007
Quality Decision Making, 2008

TABLE OF CONTENTS

Sayings	xiii
Preamble	xv
Prologue	xix
Preface	xxv
1.0 Introduction	**1**
2.0 Changing America	**9**
2.01 The Moral Character of the Free Market	15
2.1 American Greed	16
2.1.1 Coming Clean or Refusing to Admit Fault	19
2.1.2 American Values	20
2.2 American Consumerism	21
2.2.1 Audacious Consumption Epidemic	23
2.3 American Debt and Cost of Borrowing	24
2.3.1 The Sub-prime Mortgage Mess	25
2.4 Executive Pay	28
2.4.1 American Employment Practices	31
2.4.1.1 How America Lost Its Manufacturing	31
2.4.2 Skewed Salary and Reward Systems	33
2.4.3 Corruption in America	34
2.5 The New American Upper Class	35
2.5.1 American Immigration and Emigration	36
2.5.2 Economic Impact of Immigration	38
2.6 American Health Care	39
2.6.1 Improving the Quality and Cost of American Health Care	40
2.6.2 Wellness Care	43
2.6.3 America's Drug Problem	45
2.6.4 Curbing National Obesity	48

	2.6.5	The Future of U.S. Health Care	50
2.7	America's Infrastructure Management		52
	2.7.1	Managing Large Projects and Disasters	54
	2.7.2	Hanging Wires, Cables, and Pipes	54
	2.7.3	America's Response Preparedness	56
	2.7.4	U.S. Mail Service Dilemma	57
	2.7.5	American Incompetence and Arrogance or Mismanagement of Disasters	58
2.8	America's Education System		61
	2.8.1	The New For-Profit Education Systems and Sub-prime Crisis	64
	2.8.2	Rebuilding America's Education	66
2.9	America's Agriculture		68
	2.9.1	Agricultural Performance	69
2.10	Crime and Punishment in America		71
	2.10.1	American Justice	71
	2.10.2	Frivolous Use of the Justice System	72
	2.10.3	Range of American Lawyer Activities	74
	2.10.4	Rewards and Punishment	75
	2.10.5	Lobbying in America	77

3.0 American Economy — 79

- 3.0.1 American Economic Developments — 84
  - 3.0.1.1 America's Do-it-yourself Economy — 86
  - 3.0.1.2 Government Intervention in the Free Market — 88
- 3.0.2 Managing America — 88
- 3.0.3 Labor, Employment, and Productivity — 89
- 3.0.4 American Tax Collection Shortfalls and Government Waste — 90
- 3.0.5 Honesty in Marketing and Advertising — 92
- 3.0.6 Prevention versus Correction — 93
- 3.1 American Capitalism — 94
  - 3.1.1 Fair Taxation — 95
  - 3.1.2 New Approach to Capitalism and Free Markets — 96
  - 3.1.3 American Lollipop Economics — 98
- 3.2 American Corporate Welfare — 99
  - 3.2.1 Institutional Business — 101
- 3.3 America's Energy Greed — 102
  - 3.3.1 American Oil Production — 107

| | | 3.3.2 | Carbon Trading as an Environmental Benefit and Economic Boom | 108 |
| | | 3.3.3 | American Alternative Energy Developments and Acceptance | 110 |

4.0 Fixing America's Economic, Social, and Strageic Problems — 113
- 4.1 Loss of Technological Leadership — 117
  - 4.1.1 American Transport — 119
- 4.2 Who is an American? — 120
- 4.3 Military Might Alone Does Not and Cannot Assure America's Prosperity — 122
  - 4.3.1 The Rise and Fall of Great Powers — 122
- 4.4 Who Will Rule the World in the Future? — 123
- 4.5 Does the World Want America to Lead? — 125

5.0 Saving America — 127
- 5.1 Solving America's Problems and Saving Its Future — 130
- 5.2 Saving America's Agenda — 132

6.0 Rebuilding America — 135
- 6.1 Rebuilding America's Education — 136
  - 6.1.1 Primary and Secondary Education — 138
  - 6.1.2 College Education — 139
  - 6.1.3 Economic Impact of the Skewed American Education System — 140
- 6.2 Rebuilding America's Law Enforcement System — 143
- 6.3 Economics of Fair Taxation — 144
- 6.4 Balancing the Budget and Paying Off the National Debt — 145
- 6.5 American Wealth — 148
- 6.6 Savings Formula — 149

7.0 Conclusions — 151
- 7.1 The Issue of World Over-population and Our Demographic Riddle — 151
- 7.2 America's Future — 152
- 7.3 Final Note — 157
- 7.4 Rebuilding America — 157
- 7.5 Plan for America's Revival — 158

Appendix A:	How the Financial Crisis Was Engineered	159
Appendix B:	How Would the World and We Know How Great, Smart, Rich, and Good We are if We Would Not Tell Them?	161
Appendix C:	Employees of the U.S. Government (2007)	163
Index		167

LIST OF TABLES AND FIGURES

Table
1 America's Economic Slowdown
2 Global Mortgage-based Securities
3 Selected Foreign Exchange Reserves and Sovereign Wealth Funds
4 Incentives for Improving Education

Figure
1 World Export of Goods and Services (1950-2010)
2 America's Energy Greed

Sayings

- A free market democracy is the best form of government for a literate, law-abiding people. It is less so or even ineffective in societies of uneducated, lawless and/or largely self-serving people.
- Free market capitalism only works effectively in an honest, non-self-serving, regulated, and well managed environment in which leaders have the shareholders and public interest foremost in their minds. Otherwise which means usually strict regulation of markets and companies is required to prevent theft and resulting chaos.
- America will have to regain a sense of decency and sharing in its demands to contain the epidemic of unreasonable, unearned, and usually unnecessary consumption, designed more to feed its people' egos than their needs.
- *Americans will always try all the wrong solutions before they finally find the right one.* Winston Churchill, 1942.
- We must now choose between nationalizing all major U.S. banks and jailing all bankers and brokers and strict regulation of all banking and brokerage activities and transactions if we want to regain the American dream, leadership, and trust domestic and foreign.

Ernst G. Frankel

April 2011

PREAMBLE

The election of Barack Obama elated not only the American people but much of the world, hungry for a radical change in the world economy, socio/political structure and physical environment. It was for that reason that he received the Nobel Peace Prize before having accomplished anything except arousing the American public and exciting the rest of the world with the promise of change.

However, now two years after his election as President and both America and the world in economic and political turmoil, with two as yet ongoing senseless wars, and the world's largest man-made and mismanaged environmental disaster under his belt, a global economy not just stagnant but seriously sick, and international relations in shambles, America's reputation and claim of leadership is not only in serious doubt, but may have suffered irreparable damage. While the war in Iraq is winding down, without having achieved any of the objectives and left as a country in physical and economic ruin, without a government six months after a loudly acclaimed election, an infrastructure incapable of meeting many of its peoples' needs and a military/police barely capable of maintaining a semblance of domestic order, one wonders if America, Iraq and the West would not have been better off if Saddam Hussein were still in power not only to assure Iraq's domestic order and security, but also a meaningful counterweight to a nuclear power aspiring Iran. A weak Iraq will allow Iran to dominate the Middle East, the global oil or energy markets, and more. This in turn will enhance the influence of radical Islam which has invaded Europe and North America, and is undermining Western democracies, ways of life and freedoms.

The war in Afghanistan is even less meaningful. Here a tribal region ruled until 1973 by a king (actually the leader of the tribal leaders) who now resides in Italy with his sons, was willing to return and help unite the country. However, we insisted on setting up a puppet government with an unelected President, and are fighting not the al-Qaeda but locally grown Taliban, a largely religious movement which while it may not represent the majority is supported by a large number of Afghans.

Western style democracy is not only strange but an unacceptable system of choosing a governing structure. Tribes are not and never have been democratic peoples in a Western sense. Even American tribes did not select their chiefs by a one man one vote democratic procedure. Tribes have their own cultures developed by the needs of their environment. Western-style democracy requires well educated, law abiding and well connected peoples to work. Yet in today's Iraq and Afghanistan, as well as most other countries in the region, none of these prerequisites for a working Western-style democracy exist nor is there much of a chance for its introduction and acceptance in the short run.

Apart from Israel, there is not a single Western-style democracy in the Middle East, and Israel is an anomaly in the region. Apart from the two ill-conceived wars, America is engaged in an unsustainable economic misadventure. Economic strategies and mismanagement, which are driving the country into increasing debt, a lower standard of living, an over-consuming, low production economy, and a government incapable of recognizing and/or dealing with our mounting dilemma. Our problems are not new but like an ostrich (bird) we have buried our heads in the sane, unable or unwilling to recognize the new realities.

If America wants to survive or re-emerge as a great power and re-establish its reputation and leadership as well as regain its economic vitality and foundation, then it may have to adopt many if not all of the prescriptions advocated in this book.

The time has come to recognize and deal with reality and emerge from our dream world. Many of the prescriptions advocated may be hard to take and some be counter to our own prescriptions of the situation and needs, but it is becoming increasingly evident that unless America changes its ways and acts decisively soon, the world our children inherit will be markedly different and certainly not to our liking.

There is little time left to act and we must, without delay, not only change policies but also prepare our own people for the radical changes that will be necessary and/or imposed on us in the near future. We must recognize that we are no longer the best and/or the greatest, and assure that our leaders, managers, and teachers reintroduce some self recognition, humility, and self-discipline. We are still good at many things and best at some, but surely we do not lead in or own everything.

We as a people will have to learn some humility, self-discipline, and frugality. Learn to recognize our strengths and our disabilities. We will have to learn to live within our means and learn from others how to do and manage things better. Most importantly, we will have to recognize the truth and realities; otherwise, we will continue to dig an ever deeper hole from which there is no escape. The Greeks, Romans, Ottomans, and other leading powers also felt that they were invincible, best, and most effective only to fall prey to their own misled self-perception.

Let us look into a global mirror, face the truth, and start to correct what is wrong, unsustainable, and unacceptable, and get back on track. This book presents both a mirror of America and suggested prescriptions for correcting our ills and reestablishing our greatness.

Prologue

Since World War II America has not only lost much of its preeminence in science, technology, standard of living, institutional effectiveness, and even status, but while it still remains the world's preeminent economy, military power, and leads the world in foreign trade, technology development and use. Its eminent position in many fields is gradually eroding and may soon vanish. It has become the world's largest debtor with an economy largely led by and dependent on consumption and a declining or eroding industry as well as agriculture output.

America's comparative productivity position is at an historic low and is even surpassed by that of many emerging economies. America's economy has in recent years, as noted, been largely driven by emphasis on consumption and services which now comprise the bulk of its GDP and can no longer cater to most of its needs. Unfortunately, an increasing percentage of its GDP consists of consumption of foreign produced or grown goods and services. America's trade deficit is growing and with it its foreign debt. Even recent stimulus payments to citizens to restart the economy by providing taxpayers with a one-time cash disbursement only increased America's foreign debt as most of the money spent by citizens was for foreign imports, primarily from China thereby causing a direct transfer of U.S. government stimulus funding to our foreign debt. America's foreign debts are rising at an unprecedented rate and serving that debt consumes an increasing percentage of the government's budget and GDP.

Today many of the products bearing American labels, such as GE, etc. are actually produced or assembled abroad. Similarly, many of our services are provided from abroad. Americans also pride themselves as having the world's best health care, education, and law enforcement systems. In reality, these have fallen woefully behind those of many industrial and even emerging or developing countries. Although America spends more than twice the world's average per capita on health care, education, and law enforcement, the results are actually lower quality of health care, education, and law enforcement than in most developed and many developing countries.

The reasons for this are manifold and will be discussed in detail later. However, these deficiencies impact not only on our life and standard of living, but also on our standing in the world-at-large and our future potentials for growth and influence. In fact, our ability to lead or even influence future global developments may be increasingly impaired by our lack of economic abilities and status.

America was built on human capital, mainly provided by immigrants who were attracted by the freedoms provided by its social freedoms and an environment to build a most socially effective, economically vibrant and just society which made full use of the natural riches of the land. As a result, it became a most well established and rich society able to achieve enormous wealth, standard of living, and quality of life. Among its must admired achievements was the establishment of health care, and law enforcement institutions and services which became the envy of the world.

In recent years though, these institutions have been more inefficient, often self-serving and sometimes mismanaged institutions which quite often did not primarily serve the public interest. In many cases the public had to get used to the new realities of these services. As a result, we now spend an inordinate amount of public money for these services, in both real and relative terms. In fact, we spend nearly twice as much per capita or as a percentage of GDP on health care, education, and law enforcement than any other developed country. However, the quality of these services did not improve and in fact continue to decline.

There are many reasons for this situation. However, the impact on our economy, freedoms, well being, and quality of life seems to continue to decline and affect trust in government. While much of this is due to greed and mismanagement, there are also some other fundamental issues affecting it, such as our lack of firm conviction of the role of government, legality of unbridled greed and honesty, lack of regulation, oversight and its enforcement as well as public expectation and feeling of entitlement (earned or unearned). As a result, the role of government at all levels is often left more to chance than strictly written into law. While the public and many institutions look to government for economic and regulatory guidance and support, actual involvement by government is generally abhorred and discouraged. As a result, we have a situation where government provided basic support, tax exemption, and general guidance in addition to some bail out funding, while being encouraged to stay out of providing any guidance or control of these institutions. In other words, it is a situation of taxpayer support without representation or control. Taxpayer moneys are being used to keep these institutions in operation without an effective role in their operations and management.

Considering the U.S. education system first, we lament inequalities in opportunities and quality of education but insist on local funding and management of schools. Invariably these lead to gross inadequacies as poorer areas are unable to fund their schools adequately. As a result, schools in most of America are funded differently and some may have budgets per pupil several times larger than those of others. As a result, they are not only unable to attract better teachers but also unable to provide better facilities and programs.

The same applies to higher education where again some colleges not only charge very different fees than others but have significantly larger per student budgets. Another issue is access to colleges and other higher education. For some reason, this has become not an issue of interest to learn, but prestige. As a result, today most if not all American high school graduates are encouraged to go to college independent of their interests, propensity for further learning or academics, and in fact going to college has become a class and social status issue, with those not admitted or able to go ostracized and socially discriminated.

At the same time, only a small percentage of college graduates ever make use of what they learned and in fact usually end up in jobs requiring no more than a high school education. The issue is manifold. First, young people are encouraged to waste or spend 3-5 years doing something which neither advances their opportunities in life nor costs them and the public significant resources and time they could have spent learning a useful trade for which they have an aptitude. The percentage of high school graduates going on to college in America is over twice that of any other developed country. At the same time there is an increasing scarcity of skilled workers. This economic double whammy has huge economic costs. We lose much of the working life of most people who start at age 22/23 instead of 18/19, and students actually become competent engineers, while many of the bottom ranked students ended up as high earning financial services executives. This double whammy of wasted educational expenses and student time probably costs the country 4-6% of GDP in direct and indirect costs.

Other countries solve this problem by requiring students to commit to a professional career much earlier and often at college entrance of

18/19 years of age. If America were to adopt such an approach, American college enrollment and budget requirements, this means that we loose on average 10% of the productive, lifelong working hours. At the same time, we spend nearly 12% of our GDP to fund education, of which nearly half goes to higher education and much of this is wasted in educating people who will never use or benefit from the knowledge or skill acquired in college. I have taught engineering for 40+ years to find that only about half of my former students actually practice engineering after graduation. The curious thing is that the top students stayed in engineering, while most of those who could not make it in engineering or other professions worked in financial services.

The same applies to other professional areas in which those who cannot become professional become financial experts. The increasingly destructive role of financial services and other sectors of the American economy will be reviewed and a just and effective resolution of this problem will be offered.

This book is the result of several years of studying the reasons for the rapid decline of America's economy, status, and most importantly, hope and prospects. Unlike past declines, the country has lost much faith in itself, its leadership, and most importantly its ability to return to past greatness. Much of this is due to the lack of selfless, competent, and committed leadership. It is for these reasons that the country was ready to elect an unproven, inexperienced leader like Barrack Hussein Obama president on the simple promise of change. The country needs and wants change, but change must be competent, focused, and effective. It cannot just be different. However, after about two years, this new administration has not been able to introduce meaningful change. True, it has been able to use its democratic majority in both houses to push through health care and financial regulation legislation, among others, but the ways of Washington did not change and the lobbyists still rule the country.

Health care though now more readily available and covering many previously uninsured is still burdened by an unconscionably large legal and administrative burden which adds at least 50% to costs and reduces the quality of health care. Financial regulation did not include curtailment of unconscionably large bonuses, salaries, and other rewards that fail to assure that financial exports who claim huge rewards when they succeed, but do not participate in losses when they fail. They are not required or simply refuse to put their bonuses into escrow accounts to be used to pay for losses they incurred equally often by gambling with public or client money. It is a one-way street in which only the customer or taxpayer loses and barely participates in gains made from speculations with his money.

Throughout human history, big empires and powers fell: some like Egypt and Persia, as a result of internal discord, others like Rome and the Ottoman Empires because of external challenges or attacks. America, on the other hand, is declining and losing its big power position largely because of over-indulgence, greed, and insolence. In other words, it can and should only blame itself. We consume too much, produce too little, and demand what we cannot afford. Even our intellectual or technological supremacy, once the driving force of the American economy, is increasingly being exported or lost. Yet we continue not just to live well above our means, but to consider it a god-given right to maintain the "American Way of Life" of obscenely large dwellings, meal portions, newspapers and other wasteful uses that have little to do with standard of living or quality of life, but have become simply an American Standard. We can no longer justify this type of behavior, volume of consumption, and impact on the earth. We have no god-given right to strip the earth of its resources and pollute the environment towards extinction of life and habitability.

Other nations have recognized these problems and made changes that in most cases did not affect their standard of living, quality of life, and even cultural preferences. But we must learn to live within our means which really implies to consume no more than we product or the value of our production or output allows us to afford. While solutions such as high consumption, taxes or actual restrictions on consumption (gasoline taxes, minimum number of passengers/cars) are approaches used successfully in some countries, we may require even more drastic measures and greater discipline because we must not only reduce increases in consumption but actually reduce consumption.

We face similar problems in our foreign policy and strategic positions. We can neither afford nor should we assume the role of world policemen. Not only should we refrain from trying to impose our way of life, standards, morals, and even laws on others who have different values, backgrounds, and ambitions, but as we demand the freedoms of setting our standards of living, behavior, and government so do others. Western free market economy and our consent of democracy are the result of our historic experiences and include our concepts of freedoms, human rights, and duties. Others have very different experiences and needs, and our concepts may as a result not fit their needs. We must learn not only to be more tolerant and understanding but also to share not just physical resources but ideas, ideals, and most importantly concepts of human needs and rights.

This book is an attempt to put America, its way of life, policies, and demands in focus and review where we are, what we do, and what role we play. In parallel, we will discuss how we got to where we are and who we are and if we have the right to all we expect, consume, and demand.

The world is changing rapidly in economic, social, political, and moral terms, and we better learn quickly that our role in the future may be very different from that of our past. It is no longer a world of one or two major or super powers, but one in which at least three or four major powers vie for domination. Secondly, while in the past competition was mainly driven by economic and military powers it is increasingly being influenced by moral, faith-based, and other differences that affect moral, spiritual, and political differences. We live in a new world that requires new approaches, values, and policies.

The new world of electronic communications provides access to information almost instantly to anyone in the world. It also offers a much wider and more effective transfer of ideas, information, and directives which make many traditional approaches to governing and management mute or ineffective. As a result, America will need very different approaches, internal management, motivations, and strategies if it is to maintain its position as a, if not the, leading nation.

Much of the required changes will have to come from within and our studies show that American will only be able to save itself, its way of life, standard of living, ideals, and values from within. In other words, if we want America as we know it and as what the world perceives it to be and stand for to continue, some radical changes from within will be required. Otherwise, we conclude it will continue to not just lose influence, economic, and political and military power, but also its standing and role as the beacon of democracy, human rights, law, and justice. We can only help and save ourselves. There is no one else able and/or willing to do it. The prescriptions in this book are largely difficult and sometimes costly, yet any conclusions are that they are essential remedies to save what we value in and about America.

Preface

After leading the world in science, technology, economic conditions, standards of living, strategic and military prowess, international trade, and even cultural developments in literature, music, and the arts, during much of the 20th Century, America's global leadership position is now eroding and being challenged. It may well be lost soon as the first century in the 3rd millennium advances. Much of the superb economic and physical infrastructure, institutions, services, and systems built in America during the hay days of the last century which catapulted it to the global forefront are now corrupted, outdated, dilapidated and/or in urgent need of repair, updating, and often also renewal or even replacement. Greed in financial services, addiction to consume and own beyond ability to afford while insisting on free unregulated markets controlled by self and not public interest caused a near collapse of America's financial institutions.

Lack of oversight and regulation of the financial markets, trade, and many aspects of the American economy were ideologically motivated and ignored the increasing lack of honesty, greed, self-serving attitudes, and outright corruption, particularly in financial services. In a way, it was similar to handing drug enforcement and control over the drug dealers on the erroneous assumption that they would do what was good for society, control of the markets and growth of addiction, and not their own pocket books. Yet we did not learn from the experience and even now after the disaster struck, continue to propose rewarding the perpetrators.

For example, the Bank of America which took over Merrill Lynch, one of America's leading stockbrokers, proposed to offer over 53% of Merrill Lynch analysts and traders, most of whom had a direct role in the market disaster, signing bonuses in the millions to keep them onboard; this as if these people really had a choice with layoffs in the financial services industry by the tens if not hundreds of thousands. These people should be grateful to just be allowed to keep a salaried job. In fact, the bonus system prevailing in that industry was probably the main contributor to the risk prone approach prevailing in that industry. Risk takers only endangered other people's money and never exposed themselves or did they have to partake in losses.

In other words, the investing public, including all pension funds, became play money for these people who now expect to continue these unjust and unearned rewards. In fact, most should not only be grateful to be allowed to keep a job, but to stay out of jail for mismanaging investments or defrauding investors. We need a radical change in the structure of financial services where people are only rewarded for risks taken with their own assets, jobs, and careers. What we had was a risk/reward system where the public was exposed to all the risks and the risk takers rewarded themselves, no matter what the outcome. This is not capitalism but fraud.

A true free market capitalist system relies on honest, free, non-fraudulent, transparent trading. It cannot work effectively in an environment of greed, fraud, lack of accountability, visibility, and regulation, as we experienced in recent years. High bonuses, particularly not earned by superior performance, are morally wrong, economically inefficient, and socially obnoxious.

America's economic woes are even more severe. The automobile industry, once the bailiwick of American industry and pride of American manufacturing, had all three major automakers near bankruptcy and asking for government bailout. For years they have maintained their failed business strategy, building cars people neither wanted nor appropriate for today's environmentally concerned public. They continued to be awash in unnecessary white collar workers, unproductive blue collar workers, and a sales/dealer workforce of nearly 750,000 or three times the big three employment. Blue collar worker productivity at their plants was a fraction of that achieved by foreign automaker plants in America using U.S. labor. Their incompetent self-serving management continued for years to hide behind the supposed legacy cost curtain which, while partially responsible for their high costs, did not really explain the lack of competitiveness, advanced design, effective technology, and fuel efficient products that were right for the time and wanted by the public.

It is unbelievable that American car manufacturers employ 3-5 times as many white collar people per production worker as their foreign competitors U.S. manufacturing plants. There is also little justification for employing so many people in sales and services or in supporting industries. The American automobile industry, among other major U.S. industries, needs a complete overhaul and is the prime example of why America is no longer a force in global manufacturing, the heart of a thriving economy. A large country like America cannot thrive and grow on self-serving services alone. It cannot build its wealth and maintain its standards of living on consumption alone, expecting others to finance its indulgences.

America has an old, inefficient, and increasingly ineffective transport, electric power and communications infrastructure, and an inadequate education, health care, and law enforcement system. It is lagging in manufacturing and increasingly also in many services. Its inadequate institutional systems are becoming a burden instead of a crutch to its society. While America continues to lead the world in many areas of high technology and science, it is falling seriously behind in some of the most basic areas of civilization and economic activities. Its productivity has declined and its main institutions are lacking. Similarly, human developments required for maintaining a healthy growing economy and social system are falling behind others in America now.

As noted, much of America's physical infrastructure is outdated and its management incompetent, sometimes corrupt or just ineffective. This also applies to non-physical systems such as education, security, law enforcement, and health care. Something must be done soon if America is not to slide into the role of a declining and increasingly underdeveloped economy and social system. Like the Fall of Rome and other historic developments, America has for too long been content to rest on its laurels and in self-delusion, while the rest of the world, particularly China and other Asian as well as some European countries merrily marched ahead and are now on the verge of overtaking America in many areas of modern life and economic developments.

There is little inertia in America's economic system, and infrastructure development, and this heartbeat of globalized socio-economic growth is practically at a standstill in the country. Unless we start the redevelopment of America without delay its future as a world leader is very much in doubt. It is essential to focus public opinion on these issues before it is too late and conditions become irreversible. We must remove the snug feeling of self delusion and contentment from our leaders and the public-at-large and develop new priorities and initiatives to right these wrongs so as to lead America back onto its rightful path of socio-economic, cultural, and political leadership. We must recognize that we are no longer the best, most productive or the greatest in many important fields. Neither are we the freest, most well off, best cared for and most educated.

In particular, as noted, physical infrastructure, once the pride of America and a major contributor to its economic and social growth and success has in recent years become an acute embarrassment to this nation. Infrastructure failures, ineffectiveness, and the inability to properly plan, construct, manage and maintain it now pose an acute challenge to America's claims of economic, social, environmental, and technological leadership.

We must recognize that most of our road, rail, water, sewer, electric power, wired and wireless telephone, and other distributed systems infrastructure are old and often ill maintained. They also often use outdated technology. Our ports, airports, and rail terminals are archaic, ill designed, badly run, and often in bad condition. Levees, coastal defenses, and dams often lack effective design, construction, inspection, and maintenance. In New Orleans the core of many levees had been washed out long before Hurricane Katrina hit, causing them to fail, a fact not discoverable by simple visual levee surface inspection, when seismic measurements would have readily identified the growing problem for timely remedial action. Similarly, the recent Minnesota highway bridge collapse could have been prevented by proper timely inspection and maintenance. Most of our infrastructure is 50 years old or older, uses outdated designs and engineering, and has experienced little if any maintenance, updating or repair. We do not have or use advanced infrastructure testing, inspection or maintenance management methods. Hurricane Ike caused devastation of Galveston, and surrounding areas could similarly have been reduced by better or higher floor and/or sea walls.

Performance of recent infrastructure projects such as Boston's "Big Dig", Boston's Kenmore Square bus station, New Orleans' levee reconstruction, and various dams, bridges, port and airport projects are a reminder of how far this country has sunk in its public infrastructure development incapability. Rapidly developing new economies such as China, Vietnam, Korea, Singapore, India, and more all put great emphasis not only on the timely and efficient development of infrastructure but also on effective maintenance, updating, and constant improvements of these essential systems.

I returned from Shanghai and Ningbo in Central China in July 2007.

There two cities which used to be connected by one 2x2 lane highway in 1998 when I planned their ports. Since then, this highway has been enlarged to a 4x4 lane highway, and an additional new 80 Km causeway bridge road connector with 4x4 lanes will soon be inaugurated. Large American construction firms, once global leaders in their field, are increasingly being shunned for large projects abroad because of their lack of advanced engineering, planning, and implementation capability.

Much of this may in part be the result of educational priorities given to high technology, with fewer students interested in engineering and infrastructure-type problems. In the past, significant research went into the development of materials, fabrication processes, surface treatments, material handling and forming. All this allowed America to advance its infrastructure and thereby economy and quality of life for a long time. Yet, today we are faced with a debt-ridden economy, decrepit infrastructure, and an educational system which largely trains engineering scientists and not engineers and an infrastructure badly in need of complete rework, update, and modernization. We teach logistics but not transport planning and engineering, and have as a result some of the world's worst airports, seaports, train stations, bus terminals, roads, and rail networks.

Infrastructure is the lifeblood of an economy and continued failure to address its needs will invariably lead to decline, particularly in an American economy increasingly based on services and not on manufacturing and agriculture. Unless we train a larger cadre of new, well educated, committed engineers to develop a new generation of essential infrastructure, America's economic future may well be in danger. All our competitors such as China, India, and others, train a proportionally much larger number of engineers committed to and capable of advancing their infrastructure. This will give them an enormous advantage in facing increasingly complex economic challenges.

As noted, effective infrastructure is essential for economic development, health, and competitiveness. Unless we reverse the decline of America's infrastructure, our economy may collapse as one big bubble. Infrastructure engineering offers many technically and scientifically exciting challenges and American ingenuity could again lead the world in developing a new generation of infrastructure, but this will only happen if American universities reverse their priorities and reemphasize the challenges in infrastructure engineering and develop formal programs in the field.

There are many technological and scientific challenges in the planning/design, use, and maintenance of future infrastructure that are no less exciting than those in so-called high tech areas, from advanced design to sophisticated testing, control and operations management methods.

Many of our competitors built major infrastructure in less than half the time and at less than half the cost in real terms. They increasingly dominate the global infrastructure engineering and project market, a sector in which US firms led not too long ago. Much of this is the result of lack of effectively and recently trained engineers. A parallel, yet related, issue is the lack of research and related funding for infrastructure engineering. In many Asian countries, as much as 30% of engineering research funding is for infrastructure design, technology, materials, testing, fabrication research, and that percentage is growing.

There are estimates that the U.S. will have to spend as much as $6.0 trillion or 45% of GNP over the next ten years, equivalent to $680 b/year for infrastructure repair, replacement, and expansion if it wants to remain competitive in the global economy. Unless American institutions of higher learning recognize these needs and develop required programs to train the professionals needed, America's infrastructure will continue to atrophy, its economic competitiveness decline, and political world leadership vanish.

There are similar problems in the American health care, social, legal, and educational systems. Energy generation and use, environmental protection, and provision of social services are all in need of radical improvement or overhaul. These developments post a serious challenge to America's role in the new globalized world and its claims to leadership. There are many reasons for the decline in America's role and the impending peril to its position. Greed, self-indulgence, wasteful lifestyles, and selfishness are just a few of the causes for the loss of global respect and leadership. Others are loss of character, morals, and compassion in which America led the world for long in the past. Just a few years ago America's leadership seemed unshakeable, but a rapidly growing China, India, and redeveloped Europe as well as a rapidly developing second world are now challenging America.

There is an urgent need to reevaluate and redirect the American social, political, economic, cultural, and strategic priorities and reset its goals and objectives so as to reestablish America's leadership for which its Constitution equipped it so well.

America today suffers under executive incompetence and greed, political impotence and hypocrisy, lack of social incentives, corruption in its financial and other institutions, lack of meaningful social incentives, and a vacuum of leadership. Its political leaders at the federal, state, and local levels are largely concerned with their personal ambitions and careers and not the public good for which they were elected. Once in office their primary emphasis is on being re-elected and not on fulfilling the promises on which they were elected.

America today lives largely on the account of others. Its huge and increasing trade deficit is financed by foreign creditors who are expected to accept American government and other obligations in payment, something increasingly unattractive because of both a falling value of the dollar, the huge U.S. public debt of about $12 trillion, and the declining trust in American creditworthiness. As a result, more and more of these funds are going to or are being used to buy American and other assets, such as real estate, productive facilities or other economic institutions. America has truly become a debtor society, with foreign debt at an historic high in real and percentage terms. More than $200 b of taxpayer's money is now spent every year to service our government's debt to foreigners and another $250 b to Americans.

All of this has led to a global concern about America's economic, moral, cultural, and leadership future. Increasingly global tastes and values are not driven by American examples as in the past but by those of the world, of Europe and the newly developed countries such as Japan, Korea, and now China, South East Asia, India, and some developing countries such as Brazil.

America has lost much of its claim to leadership not only because of its declining economic prowess and gradual loss of leadership in technological innovation but also as a result of its deteriorating role as an example for good, as a magnet for followers, and a protector of the weak and disadvantaged.

Its new competitors such as China, for example, have not only cheaper and more abundant labor, but also more and often better trained workers and educated professionals, such as engineers. America continuous to project its power, largely by overextending its military means, while loosing much of its economic, moral, and cultural prestige and leadership.

We are blessed to live in America, a most beautiful and resource rich country that offers near limitless opportunities and many advantages few other countries offer. But these advantages have to be nourished, believed in and supported if they are to be truly maintained and accessible to all its citizens. It must also remain a beacon and example for the rest of the world, a magnet not only for the disadvantaged, down trodden, and those with little opportunity but also a light guiding cultural, civil, and moral developments and advances throughout the world.

Yet today not only is America's economy in shambles, its international reputation tattered or very low, its finances and as a result creditworthiness at an all time low, but its spiritual, intellectual, and cultural qualities are all seriously degraded and its standing as well as credentials as a leading nation are in serious jeopardy.

America's leaders seemed to generally ignore the ominous signs of an imminent downturn, and none including the candidates for President in 2008 had a solid plan of how to extract the nation from its decline and imminent loss of leadership. They failed to present well considered, feasible, and rational plans for extricating America from the economic, political, social, and strategic morass which in financial terms rocked not just the American but also world markets in the fall of 2008. Much of this should have been predictable; yet lack of and enforcement of regulations, leaving it all up to the markets caused the huge failures of long respected financial institutions which in turn caused huge losses in the markets and loss of confidence by investors.

America is not only the most indebted country in real terms but is now more dependent on imports of energy, food, manufacture, and even services than at any time in its history, much of which is paid for with borrowed money. Outsourcing of production, services, and supplies of all sorts has not become a necessity but an addiction. At the same time, Americans have grown their wasteful indulgencies as if there is no tomorrow and the debt collector will never come. They developed an economy largely based and dependent on consumerism, an approach which as we will show must invariably lead to a decline. They are encouraged by the system to consume way above their own output and means or even need, with ready credit even for those totally unworthy of credit. The sub-prime loan disaster was not only predictable but inevitable after the large-scale unconscionable feasting by mortgage lenders. What was and is incomprehensible is how many of America's and the world's premier financial institutions could be sucked into this morass. Greed as we will see was the main culprit and has become a global addiction, though its methods often originate in the good old

USA. The blame for the dilemma in which America finds itself now is widespread, and it is amazing how so many could have been drawn into this quagmire. Like quicksand, the system invariably sucked in anyone. Now we are approaching the inevitable reckoning which America and Americans are loath to face up to. Yet, facing it they must and the result will not just be painful but last a long time as there is no easy or quick solution to such widespread self delusion. Ultimately the long term repute and role of financial institutions will have to change, regulation be imposed, and contraveners punished severely.

This book is an attempt to describe and explain what happened and how an otherwise sane, hardworking, educated, and level headed people fell into such a nationwide trap. It also explains what remedies were or could be available if Americans and their leaders were truly willing and able to bite the bullet and make hard and sometimes unpopular decisions. But such decisions will have to be made to prevent not only the utter loss of America's position and leadership but also much of its assets, resources and the superior socio-economic conditions of its people. The time for action is now, and America's new leadership must implement and not just talk about change. This includes radical change in many areas in which Americans have come to assume a birthright, such as large cars, big houses, excess consumption, and waste. Americans will have to learn how to save, live within their means, consume only what they really need, and conserve the environment.

We use nearly twice as much or more of everything as the world average per capita consumption, from food, housing, and clothing to energy. We waste much and recycle comparatively little. This is not a birthright and we must become more responsible and equitable world citizens if we want to retain our economic abilities, global respect and opportunities for our people. We must erase our self-delusions in the inherent right to consume way above reasonable or justifiable levels, particularly at the cost to others.

Unless we change, we may find that much of America may soon belong to others and the supply gates to feed our indulgences may be gradually closed. The time to act is now. The decisions will be hard and often unpopular; yet they must be made if America is to reemerge from its current peril to again become a shining example for the rest of the world.

A plan for the future of America is presented here, designed to cope with or reverse many of the negative developments which have affected it in the recent past. But time is not on our side. The failures of huge financial institutions and the down grading of American companies and much of America's physical assets is just the beginning, with more and more devastating things to come. It is time to wake up and face reality. The American way of life is no longer a birthright, and the rest of the world will soon tire of underwriting it. Then the bottom could fall out altogether and America could be faced with failures of historic magnitudes which unlike the Fannie Mae, Freddie Mac, Bear Stearns, and even AIG bail outs by the federal government could not be saved. The time to act decisively is now as credit for the world's greatest sovereign debtor is running out.

American values face increasing distortion and, as noted, the American way of life is no longer a birthright others are willing to underwrite. Americans have become a nation of consumers instead of producers and now consume $800 b/year more than they produce. Consumption is not only encouraged by its leaders as an economy enhancing "Fata Morgana" but Americans are also told that they are the most productive people, a fallacy which may be true in their consumption rate but most certainly not in economic output. America continues to borrow assuming the bill or demand for repayment will never come due. Underlying this is a national feeling of entitlement to consume without producing value to pay for it.

America is a country in denial, with wants it expects to be met without an ability or even willingness to pay for them. This has been going on for a long time, but is now coming to a head. Trade imbalances have been growing for about 40 years, with increasing percentages of the trade deficits paid for by credit mostly from other countries that use much of that money to acquire American assets. As long ago as 1979, President Carter warned of the dangers of dependence of foreign oil and trade credits. Freedom and leadership require independence from other countries.

Yet notwithstanding all of this, there is a general demand that the "American Way of Life" is not negotiable no matter who has to pay for it. This includes always wanting more even if we are not able to pay for it. Yet it is becoming increasingly clear that to preserve it will require a radical change in demands and ways to satisfy them.

Our credit system is at the base of our economic problems. We are now squandering our economic assets and in future will squander our political freedom if we continue in this manner. We are using military power as a cover up for economic problems. All American presidents in recent past have considered the use of military power or threat thereof to maintain the American way of life, leadership, and imperial presidency. Our National Security State has grown to a mammoth size but does not work or identify real threats which are increasingly within. The American Presidency has become a failure often a butt of jokes and is increasingly considered a personality of hollow arms.

The imperial presidency exists in part because Congress gives power to the executive by refusing to assume its own responsibilities. In fact, the U.S. Congress is becoming increasingly irrelevant. Democrats in Congress are not forcing change but are falling into the trap of undemocratic principles, and by often adding unnecessary budget cuts. Similarly, the nation's security has been assigned to a miniscule percentage of our population, with the rest basically playing no part in it nor exposing them to danger. Similarly, the idea that America can change the world or Middle East by military force is ludicrous and simply an expensive folly the American tax payer pays for.

This book is an attempt to explain what is happening to America, why it is happening, and what it may lead to unless there are radical changes in the way Americans live, act, and treat the rest of the world. Somehow America, the standard for the world for nearly a century, has started to lose its way and may lose its role as a world leader unless it introduces some of the radical changes advocated in this book.

In 1802, Thomas Jefferson said:
I believe that banking institutions are more dangerous to our liberties than standing armies. If the American people ever allow private banks to control the issue of their currency, first by inflation, then by deflation, the banks and corporations that will grow up around the banks will deprive the people of all property—until their children wake up homeless on the continent their fathers conquered.

1.0 Introduction

America today is more dangerously divided than at any time in recent history. While there are attempts at internal unity, the reality is that Americans now have more essential and diverse concerns than ever before. The economy, wars in Iraq and Afghanistan, terrorism at home and abroad, social and economic divides and injustices, health care inadequacy, widespread poverty, unequal education and law enforcement, the nation's role in the world—all these and more concern large numbers of its citizens.

While emerging from a near century of economic, social, political, and strategic leadership in the world, America is now a ship with little direction and scant stability. A country which consisted largely of a middle class is now a house divided between obscenely rich and many who barely make a living. America used to be a country of hard-working immigrants who made the deserts bloom, invented all kinds of technologies and advances in manufacturing, large-scale farming, mining, and building—a people with a can-do attitude and a will to work together, and to succeed. It was a most perfect union not just of states but of people from many countries and many backgrounds, a place where diversity thrived and differences were not only appreciated but used to achieve uncommon advances.

Today American unity is in tatters; its institutions are in disarray, its infrastructure obsolete and falling apart, and its leadership, by and large, in question. Its political, social, economic, and strategic primacy is now challenged by older countries and newly emerging nations as well. America appears to be asleep at the wheel, and it is failing to recognize the challenges and opportunities of the new globalized world. It now finds itself without the economic, strategic, and human resources to challenge newly emerging global giants in Asia as well as a newly united Europe and a re-emerging Russia.

Not so long ago, America had abundant resources and was, unlike European powers, self-sufficient in most and able to serve as a major source of raw materials, food, and manufactures for the rest of the world.

Today America increasingly depends on other countries for fuel, raw materials, and manufactured imports, and even relies on many foods from abroad.

Its conversion to a mainly service economy deprived the nation of many of the essential capabilities of a large world-class economy and resulted in the decimation of much of its middle class. It encouraged obscenely large incomes on one hand and an increasingly large lower-paid class on the other. The country that throughout its history was a place of unlimited opportunity has become one where an increasing percentage of the population is stuck without much opportunity to advance.

In parallel, America has become a much more inter-racially and inter-culturally tolerant society. Finally, equal rights and opportunities are gradually becoming a reality. America is changing culturally and socially, but will it be able to assure effective intermixing and mutually acceptable social, cultural, and economic goals? There is danger of growing separation instead of integration. The long-standing unity of America is in jeopardy.

For centuries immigrants who made up the bulk of America's population thrived by acclimatizing to the American way of life and by learning its language and customs. Even the defeated Indians and freed African slaves gradually adopted American customs, though discrimination continued and is to some extent even visible now. Yet in recent years a trend emerged to not only dignify but revert to the customs and language of the countries of origin. Spanish has truly become a second language in America, and an increasing number of citizens no longer are competent in English. The Mexican flag is widely flown at various holidays, and people of non-Latin origin increasingly revert to their original language and customs.

Is America becoming a country more divided than united? Recent government leaders and many politicians have been loath to recognize and deal with the social, economic, and political implications of this division. While diversity has made this country great in the past, it achieved its goals by guiding diversity towards unity. Today diversity is increasingly considered a goal in itself and American pride substituted by pride of origin. The election of the first black president is a sign that America is finally recognizing the importance of unity and the need for change.

America's standing in the world, its economic capability, and leadership ability had become suspect. A period of social and economic crisis in America and throughout the world now has to be addressed through massive investments in education, health care, and infrastructure.

The rapid rise of commodity prices such as oil, gas, and food are not only distorting the world economies, but are causing widespread hunger and other shortages. If allowed to continue, these developments will cause radical changes in global trade and standards of living which may have severe political effects, both on the West and Africa. America has been singularly unprepared for these developments and the consequences may be dire.

Furthermore, justifiably or not, America is being blamed for many of these developments, particularly the price of energy and food grains, which escalated largely as a result of the misguided encouragement and subsidization of the use of grain for ethanol production. This was a shortsighted, inefficient, and costly way to produce non-petroleum fuels. In the last few years, America has lost much of its international standing as a result of the ill-advised Iraq war and the sub-prime mortgage crisis that originated in the U.S. and has affected financial institutions throughout the world. Its trade policies were similarly counterincentive, and many of its trade agreements are being questioned; this not just regarding their fairness but also their effectiveness.

In parallel, America's education and medical institutions, once the example for and pride of the world, are now sliding into severe decline. Except for a few world-class elite ones, they are generally mediocre or worse. In fact, many so-called American institutions of higher learning are nothing but remedial high schools. Why so many American youth still aspire to college degrees is a real enigma. Most induce unwarranted expectations, waste four or more years without truly enhancing skills or knowledge, and do not lead to real professional opportunities. We are moving invariably into an era of increasing mediocrity in people, institutions, services, and government, something unexpected just a few years ago.

There are many reasons for these developments that are discussed at length in this book. Similarly, there are real opportunities for prevention or at least amelioration of this predicted decline. Yet to counteract these increasingly serious developments, difficult decisions and sacrifices will be necessary, some of which touch fundamental expectations and in fact raison d'etre of Americanism.

There have been many books and articles about America's problems and recommended solutions. Most, if not all, considered particular issues such as trade, energy, or war and their impact on America and its future. While it is interesting to evaluate the effects of major issues on America's economy, international standing, trade, and American's standard of living, issues are usually linked and impact on each other.

This book is an attempt to consider the totality of effects and evaluate how they jointly impact America and what can and should be done to correct the ills of the country. We face imminent dangers that are greater than the two world wars together. What is happening now could potentially change the position, role, lifestyle, and economy of America as well as the West at large. In fact, it will likely lead to a different world, one in which new values, concepts, and social norms rule. Much of it is the result of open and largely unconstrained globalization and also America's short-sightedness in continuing a rather self-centered and, in a way, self-defeating economic, political, and strategic policy.

At a time of justified concerns over global food and energy supplies and the impact of human lifestyles on the environment, America continues to consume many times the global average in energy, food, and other resources. This not only decreases their availability and raises the price to others but also causes huge problems with waste disposal into the atmosphere, waters, and land.

Only radical changes in behavior can be effective. These may not require a reduction in the standards of living but will demand a change in lifestyle, values, and priorities. Most importantly, it will be necessary to lead America from an economy and social structure based on consumerism and waste to one that appreciates the long-term values of quality, retention, and saving.

We will show that high health care costs and lack of universal health care access in America, for example, are not largely the result of the high costs of health care provision itself but the inefficiency, overburdening, and over-regulation of the health care system. The same applies to American education, energy supply and use, transportation, and other sectors of the American economy. In a way, America will have to face reality if it wants to maintain its positions or at least remain among the leading and prosperous nations of the world. It will have to become a more responsible and equitable world citizen and accept the fact that leadership requires being an example and involves responsibility. Most importantly, America cannot be a world leader without its citizens' respect for their own leaders, something severely challenged in recent years. America's leaders will have to be more open, responsible, and understanding, and accept the fact that the role of politics is to solve society's problems.

We will discuss the linkages and interdependencies among economic and social sectors and why America will have to reorganize itself and wean its people, enterprises, and institutions from their wasteful ways. Resources of the world are now stretched to the limit, and newly developing as well as undeveloped nations are demanding their fair share. The large price increases for energy and food experienced in 2008 are just the beginning of a new era with other shortages and price escalations to follow.

America will have to adapt to the global needs for fairer distribution and consumption of resources, which will require it to abandon its consumer-driven economy. We will discuss these issues and possible equitable solutions and show that quality of life in America may actually be enhanced by less wasteful consumption and more cooperative and competent leadership.

The American system of government is truly unique and can serve the nation well if legislators and government officials truly and selflessly perform the functions assigned to them by our founders who never envisioned a legislature largely influenced by special interests instead of truly representing the needs of the people. The same to a large extent applies to government at all levels.

The time has come for a reevaluation not of our system of government but the way government is elected, chosen, and run. As a people, Americans have earned better government and must make it more attractive for honest, competent, and committed publicly-minded citizens to run for government and not leave it up to the opportunists and people with special interests to fill many government positions. America will truly have to again become a country governed by the true representatives of the people for the people.

To achieve this and reverse the trend of largely self-serving interests by leaders in the professions, business, legislatures, and government may require new moral guidelines, better education, more organizational efficiency, and most importantly public concerns, awareness, and insistence upon true enforcement of the laws without favor.

Somehow and sometime ago, our perfect union started to go astray and was undermined by growing self-interests which now permeate most sectors of public and private life in America. These trends must be reversed to make America a true example of their fair, concerned, and compassionate world leadership.

America used its dominating economic and military powers to extend its influence throughout the world since World War II, affecting millions or billions of people, many of whom did not ask nor choose America to represent them or make decisions for them. In fact, many did and do object to America's role and are opposing it actively or passively. Radical changes in American policy, strategy, and objectives are required if it is to succeed in maintaining a semblance of leadership and an important role in the world. Not only has America lost much of its economic clout and position of strength as one of the most indebted nations, but also its strategic policies in Iraq, Afghanistan, and elsewhere have largely backfired. The American concept of democracy is not only strange but is unacceptable to most of these nations as well as to most people of the Middle East and Africa. America tries to succeed where France, the Soviet Union, and others failed miserably. Its advances are still perceived as crusades where foreign invaders are opposed by selfless patriots or Jihadists more than willing to die for their cause. And the foreign American and other Western occupiers do not just want to stay alive; they want to fight on their terms and continue to impose their lifestyle, an alien and offensive concept to these resistance fighters. It is time for America and the West to learn that these conflicts are not traditional wars or campaigns against insurrection but are instead religious, ideological, and—as a result—fanatical conflicts.

These conflicts are putting American national security in jeopardy and in reality are not protecting it from terror attacks but probably enhancing terrorists' objectives, challenges, and opportunities. America's global interventions since World War II have, by and large, all been failures and did not, as stated before, enhance America's and the West's security or its political influence.

In fact, the West has lost much of its influence and prestige in the Middle East, South Asia, and Africa, while the influence of Russia and China in particular, as well as other newly developing countries, has grown in most of these areas. It is curious that Muslim fundamentalists appear more comfortable dealing with practicing or former Communists than with Christian or other monotheistic believing Western nations. This may be because they perceive these new relationships to be solely based on mutual economic and strategic advantages without any socio-political or ideological considerations. Whether these relationships will last is hard to project, but for the time being these countries seem to prefer them to the more traditional relationships with Western countries. Russia, China, and other newly developing countries are not only considered apolitical trading partners with no ideological strings attached, but often they also offer highly attractive terms. With little or no colonialist history and single-mindedness in their dealings, these new trading partners offer unique attractions to South Asian, Middle Eastern, and African countries. These in turn, though not represented in the United Nations Security Council or major world economic group, offer the fact of numbers in the U.N. where they constitute a majority.

We are entering a new and dangerous period. American' resolve to fight terrorism and expand democracy abroad is fading. It is evident that America will only be able to retain or regain leadership by example and not dominance. It will similarly need to completely overhaul its infrastructure, institutions, and services to effectively deal with the challenges of the future.

Most importantly, it will, as Barack Obama so rightly pointed out, have to change— change its priorities, objectives, approaches, and values. This change is needed from within and without. Rewards must be earned; and neither the world nor nature owes us a living, and certainly not a living beyond what we earn or even deserve. Leadership can only be earned and maintained by example for the common good and with respect for the environment.

This journey—and the required changes to make America and the world safer, more equitable, and prosperous for all peoples—is described herewith. It is a journey with many obstacles to overcome if we are to succeed in saving America from itself and assuring its rebirth as a world leader.

2.0 Changing America

America has changed as a nation, economy, and socio-political entity since World War II. At that time, it was a distinct nation of immigrants, largely from Europe with some Africans and Asians, many of whom as mentioned before did not come to America voluntarily. Although America had governed some dependencies such as the Philippines, it did not have a colonizing policy throughout its history. It occupied Puerto Rico and the Philippines after defeating Spain early in the 20th century. Spain had colonized these lands long before America offered Puerto Rico statehood, which this Commonwealth has as yet not voted on. America entered the World Wars of the last century belatedly, yet became the major factor in their outcome.

Since the end of World War II, it has assumed the roles of arbiter and peacekeeper; this has drawn it into various conflicts, from Korea and Vietnam to the Middle East, as well as smaller ones. Yet America does not seem more secure in spite of all these involvements. America's immense military power was and is no match for terrorists, guerilla wars, or insurrections on foreign soil where the adversary has large popular support. It may have overwhelming fire power but usually lacks the ground support. American soldiers try to stay alive while they fight a political war, and their adversaries fight for an ideology and are not only willing but want to die for their cause.

America is facing a new era now, both because of new leadership and because it finds itself in a new environment to which it is not accustomed. Its economic and strategic prowess is in question as well as its approach to solving global and national problems. Terrorism, the scourge of the last 50 years, has assumed new dimensions and strengths as shown in the November 26th and 28th attacks on the city of Mumbai in India. Old methods for fighting it are no longer effective, and there is no agreement on new approaches which must be introduced. Similarly, global and particularly unreasonable American consumption is growing and is challenging the capacities of the world to meet peoples' basic needs for food, shelter, and energy.

Natural disasters in South Asia and elsewhere are on the rise in frequency and magnitude. Governments find it increasingly difficult to respond to them in an effective and timely manner. This includes America, which fell far short in responding to the Katrina, Galveston, and other disasters, and let millions down. Alternative energy sources are available, but there is as yet no determined, focused effort to develop them and replace much of our fossil-fueled energy use.

East Asia is exuding increased economic and political strength, with natural resource- poor Japan and Korea adjusting their economies to the new realities of a powerful China. Yet resource demands by the new economic giants, China and more recently India, are putting tremendous pressure on global resource supplies by driving up prices and straining world food supply.

In parallel, the older, advanced economies, suffering from a declining working-age population, particularly in America and Europe, are depending more on immigrant labor. This has economic and demographic implications and affects the socio-political balance. For instance, an increasing number of immigrants are sticking to or imposing their customs without a desire to assimilate the host country's language, social norms, and behaviors. Western countries such as America and much of Europe as well as Asian countries such as Japan, Korea, Taiwan, and China are experiencing a decline in reproduction as more and more educated people delay and reduce procreation. This in turn does not necessarily result in ultimate extinction but transformation of such civilizations, which attracts other people to fill the void and, in the long run, substitute their values and customs for those of the host.

This happened with Greece, Rome, and other civilizations in history when their increasingly sterile, secular population died off and was replaced by former serfs, immigrants, and conquerors. This new population often brought more feudal, anti-secular, and patriarchal changes, forming the base for a new Europe. Unless current trends can be reversed, America is facing similar changes and the resulting challenges, which will ultimately force conversion to a less open, less tolerant, more restrictive society.

Candidates in the 2008 presidential race all advocated for and recognized the need for change but saw the needs differently. In general, they seemed to hesitate in considering the radical changes required in many areas. Most importantly, a radical change in America's role in the world is needed; its economical, global, political and social leadership, as well as its cultural example, are lacking. Unless this is done, America may find itself wandering in the wilderness of its own perceptions with few, if any, other nations following it. It is not just globalization and the emergence of new world powerhouses such as China, India, and Russia that have affected its role. America has lost its moral and economic leadership in many areas; and the associated prestige, which in the past encouraged others to accept its ideas, ideals, and methods, are now in question.

In parallel, America is no longer the manufacturing and food production powerhouse it was; and while it still leads in many areas of technology and innovation, it had to cede leadership in many others. In the distant past, its markets fostered the growth of its own industry; now its consumers support the growth of China and other new industrial giants. This loss comes at a horrific price, not just in economic prowess, but also in world leadership and ultimately America's ability to maintain its standards of living.

In addition to its political and economic decline, America is no longer the unchallenged leader in some areas of science, technology, and most certainly infrastructure. Not only do these losses affect its economic and strategic powers but also its economic standing in the world, as shown in (Table 1), which indicates an economic slowdown.

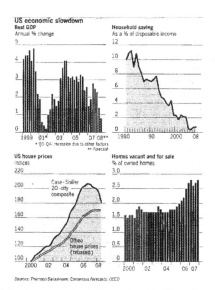

Table 1: America's Economic Slowdown[1]

---

1 Guha, Krishna and Pimlott, Daniel, "Road to Ruin? America ponders the depth of its downturn," *Financial Times*, April 22, 2008.

The economic slow down in America—largely caused by the sub-prime mortgage debacle and ineffective financial services, the housing crisis, inexcusable risk taking, waste, and mismanagement—also affected household savings, house foreclosures, and unemployment. This led to a full-blown recession in the fall of 2008. It caused large-scale failures of major financial institutions, increased unemployment, and general decline in public confidence in the American economy and its institutions at home and abroad.

Americans consider America the embodiment of democracy, social justice, capitalism and free markets. They furthermore think that their form of minimalist government and a minimally regulated economy are ideal forms of governance. It may be true that these approaches should ideally lead to a just and prosperous nation where everyone feels taken care of and provided with opportunities. This model actually worked for a long time, and America became an example of how people from all parts of the world could live in harmony and freedom and exercise their rights to choose. It was for long a land of opportunity, thereby attracting people worldwide who were dreaming of a good life, freedom, and unlimited opportunities. All of this led America to be near universally accepted as the leader of the democratic world, a beacon of hope, and proof that totalitarianism in any form is inferior.

President Roosevelt's "New Deal" was an example of how a free people could extract themselves from a largely self-imposed financial calamity. Yet now we are facing quite a different dilemma. Excesses, corruption, greed (particularly among people in financial services), combined with an overmanned largely incompetent government bureaucracy, and lack of effective regulation and accountability has led to a failure of America's and later the world's financial institutions and a breakdown of the credit system.

The lack of effective regulation, the refusal to have government intervene directly in the banking industries, and the resulting delay of the government bailout had an extremely negative effect on Wall Street and banking. All this because of a lingering fear that such intervention, even under the most dire conditions and caused by government's lack of oversight, might lead to or at least be interpreted as lingering socialism.

In other words, America's leaders would rather let the economy atrophy than be accused of interfering with free market principles. Yet the market collapse of 2008 was largely caused by lack of government oversight and regulation based on the assumption that the market knows best and that self-regulation was the best and most efficient system. These decision makers either did not expect or ignored the mounting greed, corruption, and unaccountability of the market, particularly the market leaders who had always been identified as the pillars of propriety, public consciousness, and honesty by government. The companies, firms, and institutions who invented all kinds of instruments and derivatives to bypass regulations, visibility, and accountability were also the ones who encouraged, even rewarded, risk taking and gambling with the public's funds—insolent or outright theft of investors' money.

Lehman Brothers, for example, gave Mr. Fuld, its CEO and chairman, a huge golden parachute after he drove the firm into bankruptcy. In parallel, its European manager, who was fired earlier, got a farewell present of $16 million, even though he was let go by cause. Mr. Fuld justified these payments as being part of a contract that had to be paid no matter what the cause or condition of the severance. He omitted comments on treatment of thousands of the firm's non-executive employees who also had severance agreements covering payment for unused leave, pension rights, and more. They got nothing. This is a sign of the utter lack of morals in the upper echelons of many financial institutions, including AIG, who were bailed out with taxpayers' money.

America's approach to capitalism has its lost direction. Its leaders demand that government should not be an owner, partner, or even regulator of private business, yet the same business leaders are the first to demand bailouts with public money after losing in risky gambles. And then they insist that the taxpayer and their employees should take the fall and pay for their mistakes while they walk away with ill-gotten rewards as if nothing happened.

There is really no democracy in American capitalism, with a few draining the public purse without any accounting or responsibility. Shareholders of most American companies have long been ignored by managements who account to nobody but themselves and operate a selfish, self-serving regime.

What we have is not really capitalism but a free-for-all, unregulated gambling system where the gamblers play with the public's money, cash in the gains, and dump losses onto the public. They can never lose and in fact, as noted, reward themselves win or lose. Some of our regulatory agencies such as the SEC are now an acute embarrassment.

The industry comes up with new instruments and derivatives all the time and they have in common: I win, I get the loot; lose, I get a bonus. The number of culprits who distorted and ruined America's financial system is actually quite small, but the damage they caused is huge and global. In fact, it is larger than the U.S. Government budget. Even so-called unbiased ratings of securities and insurance of financial instruments (bonds, credit default swaps, and more) are usually not just unreliable but, more often, false—and sometimes even corrupt; as a result, really a farce.

In October 2008, more than a trillion dollars in stock market value was lost in a day, and a $700 billion bailout was approved by Congress to help the financial industry get back on its wobbly feet and stop it from imploding as a result of its mistakes and gambles.

For years, Americans discredited European pseudo-socialism and South American populist socio-capitalism. They loudly proclaimed the gospel of true free market capitalism, with little or no regulation or oversight as the true path to economic success. Their claim that the market knows best and would always act in the best interest of the economy was not only proven wrong but shown to work only in an ideal society of intelligent, public-spirited, honest people, and particularly their leaders.

Other approaches to socio-economic success have in recent years proven not only more successful but also adept at dealing with social, political, and economic problems under conditions of rapid political, technical, and social change. It may well be that unfettered free-market capitalism was and is appropriate during some times and in some environments, but it is becoming increasingly clear that it not only permitted but encouraged excesses and outright fraud that hurt the economy and the public. Most importantly, it undermined the public's pocketbook and confidence in the system. In America, free-market capitalism, largely associated with "Reaganism," became an unassailable doctrine that was credited with the economic success of this country at that time.

Yet globalization masked many of its drawbacks as did the rapid conversion of America into a huge consumer society where credit was king, and ultimately its citizens as well as the nation became a credit addict. Everything was bought on credit and monthly trade deficits grew to over $60 billion. As a result, America's foreign debt, mainly to supplier countries such as China, mushroomed to trillions of dollars with an associated interest commitment. For the time being, lenders were willing to accept government obligations for their money, but lenders are becoming increasingly hesitant to accept obligations and are opting instead for real assets. Before long, we may therefore find an increasing amount of America's real assets change ownership and become foreign assets.

While the trigger for the global economic downturn of 2008, which actually started the previous December, can be traced to the American sub-prime mortgage debacle or greedy financing schemes, it soon enveloped other sectors of the financial markets and later the total American as well as the global economy. The most important factor was the belated recognition of the problem, which even then was not considered the massive dilemma it actually was. The huge and rapidly-growing U.S. debt held, as noted, mainly by China and other major exporters to the U.S. cannot be easily repaid by American exports. Debt holders will increasingly lose faith in the U.S. Government's ability to service this debt.

America is no longer the wealthiest or the most productive country. It is in debt over its head and also unable to pay for everything it needs, driving it more into debt. There is little hope that this situation will change in the short run, if at all, largely because of the misguided economic strategy of the American government, which stressed domestic consumption instead of production as the driving force for economic development. They let American manufacturing, services, and even food processing go abroad, as well as American productivity ship behind that of many other countries. This will make it difficult for America to regain its economic and strategic power.

2.01 THE MORAL CHARACTER OF THE FREE MARKET

A system of free markets not only implies an absence of government involvement and regulations but depends also on systems of laws in place. There is often a fine line between lawfulness and regulation. Markets can permit unregulated trading yet enforce property rights and others, which in effect tend to pose a degree of regulation. While free markets encourage competition, which in turn should foster efficiencies, they also provide opportunities for fraud and corruption. Free markets permit immoral behavior and value morality to take advantage of the efficiencies of free markets. As noted, while free market competition encourages efficiencies, it also offers easy opportunities for immoral, anti-social behavior.

Our founders argued that an America using free trade would prosper and grow and would encourage greater moral behavior and virtue than one enforced by sets of laws and regulations. They assumed that the opportunities offered by a free market would generate greater productivity as well as wealth and social equilibrium. On the other hand, open opportunities for unbridled profit and a singular goal of wealth and materialism in a free market encouraged greed, self-interest, and ultimately corruption.

2.1 AMERICAN GREED

Failure of the corporate financial and political systems to provide fair representation to average citizens is largely the result of the prevalence of greed throughout American society and its institutions. People at all levels of society, all the way to leaders of industry and government, increasingly break the law or act unethically for financial gain, with little concern for the law, ethics, honesty or simple decency. More and more, financial success is an excuse for anything under the guise of greed. Mortgage brokers and bankers made home loans at predatory terms to people who could not possibly afford the homes or service the loans. Then they packaged (securitized) these bad obligations with a handful of better quality ones and sold these packages to greedy bankers or investors worldwide who only considered the high return but not the risks. While most buyers were American institutions, many foreign venerable banks were also sucked into these scams (Table 2).

Top 15 companies	Holdings in $ billions
JPMorgan	49.9
Credit Suisse	41.7
Bank of America	34.7
Lehman Brothers	33.5
RBS	30.8
Morgan Stanley	30.0
Deutsche Bank AG	30.0
Barclays Capital	23.9
Citibank	22.4
Alliance & Leicester	21.0
Merrill Lynch	20.9
UBS	16.4
Goldman Sachs	13.1
Countrywide	9.0
BBVA	7.9

SOURCE: Thomson Reuters
GLOBE STAFF

Table 2: Global Mortgage-based Securities

As shown in Table 2, global mortgage-backed securities held by the top 15 companies amounted to close to $500 billion according to Thomson-Reuters (September 2008). Adding the direct holdings of sub-prime mortgages by brokers and others, as well as the holdings of smaller companies, the total sub-prime exposure would globally exceed more than $1.5 trillion dollars by mid 2008. Securitized sub-prime mortgages became one of the principal profit drivers for financial firms in the last few years; and until the multi-trillion dollar bubble burst, investment bankers continued these trades, although the handwriting was on the wall.

Investment banking rewards its financial analysts, investment professionals, and others with a two-tiered system, a stable base salary and a variable incentive called the bonus. The latter varies from year to year and is supposed to be a function of the performance of the employee. Bonuses are supposed to be typically paid out in cash, though a smaller fraction could be distributed as equity. Bonuses are a sign of the success of the employee's contribution to the firm and therefore shareholder's value. Yet in recent years, the cost of bonuses has frequently exceeded dividends paid to shareholders and often has been received independent of a measurable contribution to the firm's success. The bonus system puts all risks on the shareholders as the employee can never get less than a zero bonus, even if he contributed huge losses. In fact, bonuses are usually paid even if the firm loses. This reward system causes employees to take undue and often huge risks at the shareholder's expense, and it played a major role in aggravating the sub-prime mortgage debacle.

Many have questioned why CEOs and other executives of now failed financial institutions who gambled investor's and depositor's funds to pad their bonuses should receive golden parachutes while those who lost their investments are left high and dry. Considering that they—unlike a gambler who uses his own funds—are using funds of others, did their misdeeds usually without the knowledge and consent of the owners. They should be rewarded for their greed and misdeeds, and properly so, by prison. They are no better than thieves in the night that used their position and the public's trust to feather their pockets and their benefits. We unfortunately do not have gulags for such gamblers who, in a way, are greater public enemies than common criminals.

Much of the recent financial downturns were due to lack of government oversight and enforcement of regulations. Some of these financial shenanigans, such as the use of sub-prime mortgages, overwhelmed the market and should have been discovered, controlled, or stopped by proper application of existing regulations. In fact, there are adequate regulations in place for many of these developments but few are effectively enforced.

During the September 2008 meltdown when the credit crisis hit Wall Street and world markets causing declines of 4-6 percent per day, some surviving financial institutions resorted to large-scale illegal short selling and generally got away with it at a huge cost to the investing public, taxpayers, and government. Lax regulation and enforcement have fed and even supported greed.

Risky derivatives were similarly used to profit at the expense of the general investor public. Other examples of greed and gouging abound. For example, Hurricane Ike hit Houston on September 12, 2008, and damaged some of the U.S. refineries as well as causing massive destruction to urban and coastal communities in southern Texas. The major concern of newscasters was not loss of life and property but the resulting increase in the price of gas. When damage to the petroleum infrastructure, if any, was yet unknown, gasoline prices skyrocketed first in southern Texas and then across much of the country. Similarly, U.S. financial markets showed that traders and markets respond to speculation and not the result of events. They speculate on events, gouge the public, and run with the profits; and these are often unearned because often there is little to no damage necessitating price increases.

In many other markets, price increases must be justified by increasing costs, but not in America. While unjustified increases are mostly experienced in the retail oil markets, it also happened in the food markets when large food price increases were "justified" by the demand of products such as soy and palm oil for bio-fuels. According to the U.N. Food and Agriculture Organization, between 2003 and 2007, food prices including those of oils and fats increased by 250 percent while the portion used to make bio-fuels increased from 1-7 percent. World consumption grew from 124.6 million tons per year to 152.3 million tons per year, changes that hardly justified the price increases.

Among the most obscene rip-offs and signs of greed in America is the luring of the elderly into putting all their money into so-called indexed funds or annuities, which not only have huge sales charges but also very large early redemption fees often hidden in the fine print. Deceptive practices and tricks of the trade may include selling a 75-year-old an annuity or a type of indexed fund with cash redemption penalties starting at as much as 20 percent and only going to zero after 15-20 years or when the person is 95 years old. In other words, if the person dies before then, the insurance company and its sales agent get a huge payout. There is even a training institute called "Annuity University" that trains agents how to trick people, particularly seniors, into buying rip-off instruments. Security brokers of so-called reputable firms such as Merrill Lynch, Prudential, and others are no exceptions. They often recommend securities of firms they know are on the verge of bankruptcy or "re-establishment."

2.1.1 Coming Clean or Refusing to Admit Fault

Living up to horrible mistakes or losses by senior bankers who gambled their investors' and depositors' funds has not only been difficult, but most tried to refuse to recognize the problem and, even more importantly, their role in it. The departure of the CEOs of Merrill Lynch, Citibank, and others in the fall of 2007, usually with handsome retirement packages, showed how self-serving the financial industry had become. In every case, the institution had lost billions of dollars with much more to come. Its share value plummeted and its investors as well as depositors ultimately took the fall. There was no real admission of culpability. They gambled and the investors lost.

More recent developments in cleaning up the mess increasingly involve the federal government, which is ominous unless supported by more effective and imposed regulation. The bailout of Bear Stearns with taxpayer money with J. P. Morgan taking few risks is just one example. The banks made tens of billions in the sub-prime mortgage debacle and by trading funny types of securities without fully informing investors of the risks. The whole fiasco was one big speculation by banks and their brokers who took the general public, borrowers, and investors for one long ride; and now they expect the taxpayers to help bail them out. Wall Street made lots of money in creating and selling securities they knew were not just risky but bad and sold them to the world at large, undermining the global financial system. It is unbelievable that many in the industry, which has fought regulation and always emphasized the quality of internal oversight, now expect the government and ultimately the taxpayer to step in and bail them out. They obviously want to keep the loot and let others take over largely worthless securities. Wall Street in a way developed its own unregulated banking system, something that should not be allowed. The utter lack of transparency and information on the risky mortgages or other assets supposedly backing them up borders on criminality.

Since today large financial firms are closely interlinked, failure of one could have a cascading effect not only on national banks and institutions but also the global financial industry. In 1998, the Fed organized the bailout of the nation's premier hedge fund, "Long Term Capital Management," which had more than a trillion dollars worth of outstanding transactions with other institutions and was on the verge of going under. To assure the markets, the Fed has introduced new approaches to provide the industry with large amounts of short-term funds to the tune of more than half a trillion dollars. Ultimately, the taxpayer is footing the bill for this unreasonable risk-taking and the folly of the financial institutions who were only concerned with profit and self-enrichment of their executives and senior staff.

The near failure and subsequent bailout of AIG, the world's largest insurer and financial services provider, by the government which used $80 billion to take over an 80 percent share of the company as a cash infusion is just one example. Yet the executives gave themselves a $440,000 retreat to a resort, at taxpayer's expense, as a reward for their incompetence.

2.1.2 American Values

"Americanism," for many, implies freedom in all respects—a concept which, while idealistic, is not very practical at a time when people do not generally share idealism as a concept or a belief. It was something our forefathers thrived on that, to a large extent, is embodied in our Constitution. Yet it's something that only works and maintains harmony and progress when it is accepted and practiced by people at large.

In reality, America today is very different from that of our forefathers and the writers of our Constitution. It is still a country of immigrants yet one that increasingly transfers the burdens to others. We continue to claim leadership in most areas of modern life and economy but depend more and more on others to not only pay for it but also to carry the burden of controlling it. Among the examples is the control of drugs; for long we insisted on controlling the supply, with little effort at constraining the demand.

A most basic rule of human behavior is that any demand, particularly if someone is willing to pay dearly, will be filled by supply. Furthermore, while demand is under our own jurisdiction, supply can never be effectively controlled by us. Physical border restrictions, foreign arrays, and pressure of foreign governments never work over the long run and usually backfire. Yet this is exactly the policy we have pursued with little success. In fact, most of our efforts be they in Bolivia, Colombia, or even Afghanistan, actually backfired.

The time has come to reevaluate the approach. Although I do not advocate a Singaporean method—outlawing possession of drugs (for use or trade) at the penalty of death—there are reasonable ways drug use, domestic distribution, and trade can be discouraged. This would vastly lower our health care costs, increase productivity, reduce crime and prison occupancy, and enhance American influence and standing abroad. There is a need to crack down on the domestic drug distribution and use system. Drug trading as well as use must be prosecuted, with punishment by treatment and exposure for first-time users and criminal punishment for dealers, distributors, transporters, and habitual users, the latter only after repeated treatment. Americans are always being told that they are the best and have it best. These assumptions are never questioned even if contradictory facts hit your face.

Productivity in America is always presented as being superior to that of almost all other countries, though it is easily shown that others require fewer man-hours to build an equivalent car, ship, TV, or most other products. Furthermore, we usually omit our huge and largely unjustified or wasteful white collar and related overhead. The same applies to many of our services which, while some are superb, on average fail to make it work. In America, for example, highly complex diseases and other ills or accidents are well treated, yet run-of-the-mill diseases or accidents get perfunctory or no treatment.

2.2 American Consumerism

For several decades now, the American consumer accounted for the bulk (up to 70 percent) of the American Gross Domestic Product (GDP). In fact, politicians of all shades try to win consumer support and credit for encouraging consumers to spend even more. Never mind that an increasing percentage of purchases are imported or at least much of the material or components used in their manufacture come from abroad. This used to be so for simple cheap toys, appliances, and clothing but now increasingly encompasses all kinds of goods from toys to complex electronics, cars, expensive clothing, and even pharmaceuticals and food.

In fact, there are few categories of goods that are not imported at least in part. Similarly, many American-made goods and products have increasingly large foreign components or use foreign-made materials. As a result, the economic contribution of the American consumer to the American economy is rather nebulous, particularly as the American trade imbalance continues to grow and now (2008) is well above $600 billion or about 4 percent of the American GDP.

More than half of all American imports are bought on credit, as the value of exports in recent years covered less than half the cost of imports, notwithstanding the declining value of the dollar, which supported growth of exports.

America used to be the world dominant producer and exporter of food. No more; and an increasing amount of raw and processed foods are imported. Similarly, many components and materials used to manufacture American goods are now imported for final assembly and manufacture in the U.S., including auto parts, food, and pharmaceuticals.

Americans consume nearly twice as much of everything as the world average, from clothing and food to energy. As a result, they also discard nearly twice the world average, so consumerism in America adds significantly to waste disposal. Americans, on average, use goods such as appliances, cars, and clothing for much shorter periods than most and usually discard them long before they are worn out.

Consumerism has many side effects apart from waste, foreign indebtedness, and environmental pollution. It also impacts on social structure and behavior. People often shop for entertainment rather than to fulfill some needs. They often buy on impulse and later find little need for the purchase. This also contributes to waste, as many of these purchases are discarded often before even being used.

American consumerism has been touted as a major stimulus, but really it has a number of implications for the American economy that are not positive. Apart from the fact that it encourages waste, it also wastes time and diverts people from other more stimulating, educational, and healthy activities. Pushing consumption ultimately reduces people's development—they are under the undue and often dominating influence of advertising, marketing, and sales. It also reduces people's physical activity and intellectual stimuli. Americans spend more time than any other people shopping, which for many has become the principal leisure-time activity. This is not only wasteful but also reduces physical and mental output or productivity, as by its nature it is designed to help make decisions for people.

As noted, investment banks not only took on more risks but gambled on unknown and highly unreliable investments, which were really not investments but simply leveraged games with largely expected losses. They simply fed American consumerism into the housing market by expanding equity consumer funding and mortgages credit to unworthy borrowers who purchased real estate they could not afford or used that funding for purchases. Providing mortgages with little or no money down is not only irresponsible but counterincentive. Many of these new buyers used excess funding, as well as the government incentives, not for investments but purchases of imported goods, which made trade deficit worse.

2.2.1 Audacious Consumption Epidemic

Most people in the world shop because they want or need to have something, whereas Americans often shop for pleasure, entertainment, or to have what is being newly offered. Shopping in America is largely a social activity and a way to spend time. As a result, a significant amount of food, clothing, toys, and even appliances are purchased but seldom used. In fact, dumps in America often contain huge numbers of hardly used articles, food, supplies, and more. Shopping as entertainment drives merchants to offer goods that do not meet particular needs but are interesting and colorful. American's consumption is really outrageous in terms of quantity and choices. Because much goes unused, the waste and disposal costs are often high in environmental as well as economic terms.

Because repair of many items often costs more than replacement, there is also a built-in waste in the system caused by marketing strategies. For example, printers and fax machines are very cheap since the seller expects to profit not from the sales of the devices but from the sales of ink and other consumables required by the device. As a result, people will often buy several printers because the machine is very cheap, often costing less than replacement of ink cartridges. The same applies to many other items such as computers, monitors, and more.

American restaurants are renowned for the size of portions served, and practically any restaurant will provide doggie bags to take unconsumed food home. But waste goes much further; it is prevalent in industry, services, construction, and government. In fact, many policies encourage huge waste. For example, the U.S. Postal Service offers very low rates to marketing services while charging exorbitant rates for normal postal deliveries. As a result, the amount of marketing and publicity material has mushroomed. On a typical day, I might discard 80-90 percent of deliveries without even opening them. The huge costs to the postal service as well as the environment are not considered but are borne by the public. A reverse incentive to reduce junk mail should be introduced where junk mailers are not subsidized but bear the full cost of the postal services provided. We could then probably reduce or eliminate postal service deficits, improve the services, and save millions of trees per year.

2.3 AMERICAN DEBT AND COST OF BORROWING

Americans have driven up their debt to a dizzying $14 trillion. In other words, outstanding U.S. household debt exceeds the national gross product. The American economy has for some time now been supported or even driven by the American consumer. Yet this consumer financed much of his purchases by debt and much of this debt by debt to foreigners. In other words, the American economy is largely sustained by foreigners.

Consumer finance is largely provided by home equity and credit card borrowings, both of which expose the consumer to inordinate risks. Borrowings against the equity in the home assumed that home values would forever rise and therefore homeowners could borrow essentially against the increase in home values without risking foreclosure. This is exactly what many Americans did.

In parallel, the sub-prime mortgage market introduced large numbers of non-creditworthy people to home owning, which they could not afford. And furthermore, they could not sustain any risk of declines in house values because they usually had little equity in the home to start with; or they had borrowed against whatever equity they had, often up to 100 percent of the market value of the home. Any home value declines immediately put them into a foreclosure mode. In addition, many of the same people used credit cards to finance not only purchases but also home-owning expenses. Such cards with predatory interest rates of 20 percent plus immediately exposed them to a debt spiral.

Americans carry more average debt than most and far outweigh any people in the amount of under-secured, mainly credit card, debt. They seldom use cash and usually have a number of credit cards that were offered through the mail with various incentive programs. In fact, because the competition among credit card issuers has become very intense, issuers try to lure users with ever more attractive incentives. As a result, users often have combined credit card lines that far outweigh a rational borrowing line for them. Yet the attraction of ever-ready credit encourages users to over-extend themselves, a major reason for the huge debt exposure of the average American consumer. Adding these obligations to mortgage, car, and other loan debts often burdens people beyond their ability to service their debts.

This has become a serious problem for Americans who in recent years were lured into predatory mortgage loan contracts they could not afford. Lenders and borrowers both played with the assumption that ever-rising home values would assure a safe margin. Yet once the overbuilt housing market bubble burst and home values stopped rising, borrowers found themselves not only with debts they had difficulty serving but also asset values lower than the outstanding mortgage debt. In parallel, they were often exposed by high credit card charges, particularly when only paying monthly minimums. The combined effort resulted in the huge credit crisis of America in 2008.

2.3.1 THE SUB-PRIME MORTGAGE MESS

The American economy was shocked by one of the greatest financial losses in recent time; one that without radical intervention could drag it not just into a recession but into depression and take much of the world's economy with it. The culprit was a mortgage lending scheme by which non-creditworthy borrowers were induced into financing home purchases they could not afford, with little or zero down payment and predatory, usually adjustable, mortgage rates. The mortgage brokers induced usually unsophisticated, simple-minded, often poor people into such schemes with the assurance that rising home prices would soon give the borrower real equity in the no-down-payment house; and this would allow him or her to readily finance the loan. However, the loan would usually increase rapidly from a low to a predatory rate of interest that the homeowner could not afford.

Mortgage brokers placed these mortgages with millions of low- or no-income families and then securitized most of them by bundling such high-interest-rate mortgages with a small number of higher quality mortgages to give the impression of a high-quality securitized mortgage loan package. These were then sold to investors all over the world. By early 2008, the securitized prime mortgage papers outstanding in the U.S. were in the hundreds of billions, with an equal if not greater amount outstanding in the rest of the world. Altogether sub-prime mortgage investments were estimated to exceed a trillion dollars; they could grow to nearly twice as much if other critical mortgages were included.

Critical mortgages here were assumed to be mortgages where outstanding mortgage debt exceeded the market value of the underlying home in the declining market. Home markets continued to tumble as more homes were foreclosed and put on the market, causing home prices to tumble causing even more homes to be foreclosed and so on. Banks and other financial institutions who greedily had purchased these very risky high interest "mortgage backed" securities (many of which went into default soon after placement) were now in dire financial trouble and had to cover losses of tens of billions of dollars from reserves, borrowings, or government bailouts.

The sub-prime problem not only depressed the U.S. and some European housing markets and cost hundreds of billions of dollars in losses largely assumed by banks and other financial institutions sucked into this morass; but it may, as pointed out by Samuelson,[2] have consequences way beyond housing losses and the large decline in the dollar value. It may, for example, cause major defaults in "Credit Default Swaps" (CDS), a commonly used insurance contract on loans or bonds that pays lenders all or part of the loan if a borrower defaults. The volume of CDS has increased greatly since 2004, about sevenfold. If CDS investors or issuers were themselves to default (a real possibility) and sub-prime mortgages and similar loans were to lose their insurance coverage, the whole problem would be even further magnified.

Housing equity has for long been the major asset of most Americans and certainly of the working and lower middle class. The loss of about $4 trillion in housing equity puts a large number of Americans at risk of not being able to maintain their standards of living, pay for college, have effective retirement financing, and other important obligations. Housing inventory would ultimately lead to the bursting of the housing bubble; and there was immediate default of huge numbers of borrowers, particularly those who got adjustable predatory zero-down-payment mortgage loans. The American housing market is now valued at 4

---

2   Samuelson, Robert J., "A Sequel to the Sub-prime Mess," *Newsweek*, December 24, 2007.

percent of GDP, over half a trillion dollars, and about one-third of the value of U.S. exports.

Three million homeowners were projected to default on their mortgages in 2008 or about 5 percent of outstanding mortgages. The major problem was that as noted the mortgage market changed radically in the last ten or more years. Instead of most mortgages being direct contracts between borrowers and lenders, mortgages were lumped together and securitized to be sold off to third parties with no knowledge of the borrower or the markets in which money was lent. Even though the Federal Reserve has had the authority to prevent irresponsible mortgage lending since 1994, it did not use it to control the mortgage market.

Representative Barney Frank,[3] in an interview with *Money* magazine, describes how the sub-prime mess resulted from lack of regulation, large-scale securitization of mortgages, greedy mortgage lenders and homeowners, home market speculators, and misled homeowners. By and large, it was one large deception with everyone relying on the continuation of the housing bubble, which would escalate house values into safe profit margins. But the system encouraged such a large escalation in home ownership and the housing inventory that, once the bubble burst, the whole house of cards collapsed with it.

The resulting fall in house values caused huge numbers of houses to be worth less than their outstanding mortgages. Furthermore, many of the mortgages were adjustable with low initial teaser rates and outrageous follow up rates of 11-18 percent per year. With massive foreclosures and more expected, lenders are being asked to modify lending terms and rates that borrowers can service. The old assumption that every American could and should be a homeowner and pushing them into obligations they could not afford was a huge speculation that turned upon itself. To get out of this mess, which not only became a major factor in the decline of the U.S. but also much of the global economy, the Federal Housing Administration will guarantee mortgages against default as long as lenders modify mortgages to loans that are no more than 90 percent of the homes' current market values. Under such conditions, homeowners should be able to refinance with more reasonable terms. This approach, which may cost lenders some money, is expected to stabilize the U.S. mortgage market.

While the costs to the American taxpayer for this approach may be as high as a few billion dollars, it is expected to prevent a wholesale debacle

---

3   Interview with Representative Frank, *Money*, September 2008.

of the housing market, stabilize the mortgage market, and greatly reduce future foreclosures. In addition, we obviously need greater oversight and regulation. Basically, this approach is to induce lenders only to lend to people who can meet their payment obligations independent of variations in the housing market; in other words, to prevent large-scale speculative lending and transfer of low-quality mortgage assets to unsuspecting investors.

2.4 EXECUTIVE PAY

In the last 30 years, American corporate executive pay has risen out of all proportion to corporate performance or profit, particularly in the financial sector of the economy where pay and bonuses have assumed obscene levels. And this has happened independent of the economic or political state of the nation. A recent study by compensation experts found that, on average, CEO pay in large industrial companies rose by an average of 15.1 percent per year during the last decade and by appreciably more in financial firms. As a result, today's executive pay in America bears no relationship to the executive's performance, the firm's stock price or profitability, or the pay of employees.

Corporate boards, and particularly compensation committees, have become increasingly beholden to CEOs and can—as well as will—always find ways to compensate him or her. There is an urgent need to reform the system and make boards more responsive to owner's/stockholder's interests. They may require board members to truly stand for election by shareholders in a way that would allow them to be voted off the board if they do not represent shareholders' interests. One approach advocates that CEOs and other senior executives be rewarded with restricted company stock in addition to a reasonable base pay, which would tie the value of their reward largely to company or stock performance.

Boards must be prevented from circumventing shareholder interests and directives and real punishment or disincentives provided to assure compliance, including criminal charges for malfeasance. While CEOs of the 500 largest American companies earn 88 times the average pay of their employees, this ratio is less than 18 in Japan and other advanced Asian economies. Also Europe lags far behind the obscene non-performance related rewards of American chief executives. But the problem continues down the line as other executives and even analysts and brokers in financial firms are rewarded with huge bonuses that bear no relation to their firms' or their own contributions.

All of this distorted pay not only undermines the performance of American firms but also the morale of their workforce, who more often than not are the first to be laid off when a company's performance lags. It also makes American business less competitive globally, more expensive than necessary at home, and undermines economic growth. Many of my graduate students in science and engineering ended up in high paying jobs in finance and related industries. It is curious to note that those who could not make it, and had performed badly in their true profession—science or engineering, ended up in financial firms and made a bundle.

Notwithstanding the increasing credit crunch, financial losses, and turmoil in the stock market; American executives—particularly in the financial service sector—continue to collect obscene salaries, bonuses, and other compensation. Income inequalities in the U.S. are increasing so rapidly that already obscene levels of direct and indirect compensation of executives is becoming ridiculous by any standard. It is now hundreds of times that of an average company employee in the 1000 largest companies in the country and several times that in various financial institutions. Most ridiculous is the fact that compensation appears to bear no relationship to performance, and failed executives who are let go or forced out after collecting their ill-gotten "rewards" usually leave with a golden parachute and are hired by other firms at a comparable remuneration level. This is particularly ludicrous when considering that executives of most foreign companies in the same field, with whom the American firms are supposed to compete, receive a small fraction of the compensation of their American counterpart.

The average compensation of Japanese executives in the 1000 largest firms in their country is about 16 times the average remuneration of their employees. Even the largest Japanese, Korean, Singaporean, and other Asian companies in manufacturing, trade, or finance do not reward their senior executives—including their chief executives—with anything like the obscene payments received by their American counterparts. This also applies to CEOs that are or were founders and major shareholders or investors in the company.

At U.S. Congress committee hearings in early 2008, recently "retired" titans of American corporations were chastised as examples of excessive unearned executive compensation; while their shareholders lost huge amounts of money, many of their employees lost their jobs and their customers were often ill-served. With financial troubles, credit problems, and market turmoil abounding, executive pay continued its ludicrous upward spiral at a time of severe economic troubles in the U.S. and the global marketplace.

America's income inequalities are particularly alarming because the country claims to be an economic, social, and cultural leader and would like to be the example of a free market democracy for the world. The major effect of this enormous income inequality has been the decimation of America's vibrant middle class, the mainstay of its economic development. While the poor are largely supported by government safety nets, there is little if any help available for the middle class; and this particularly affects the lower or just emerging middle class in America, traditionally consisting of the most productive workers in manufacturing, agriculture, and services.

On average, the CEO of a Standard and Poor (S&P) 500 company in America received total compensation, including stock options and other benefits of $11.5 million in 2007 according to Reuters' estimates. This is significantly more than some of the most successful European and Japanese executives obtained. In 2007, the median income of an S&P 500 CEO nearly doubled, while the average profit of their companies rose by a measly 12 percent. Most importantly, in America, executive pay has grown at double digit rates, sometimes by as much as 50 percent per year during the last few decades; while workers' pay has been practically stagnant. Similarly, while the ranks of executives and their rewards continued to grow independent of corporate performance, workers increasingly lost their jobs and benefits during company and economic downturns.

At the same time, investors, the real owners of these American companies are increasingly losing their voice in company matters and are playing a more and more passive role imposed on them by management. Boards largely appointed by the executives are often beholding to management, and they reward executives with obscene pay packages not for their performance but for appointing board members to their own lucrative and prestigious positions. The traditional argument is: for true capitalism to be successful, entrepreneurialism must be nurtured by large rewards to executives, as suggested in an article in the *Financial Times* by Francesco Guerrera.[4] Yet few American executives

---

4   Guerrara, Francesco, "Gentlemen, Please Empty Your Pockets," *Financial Times*, March 25, 2008.

have introduced successful entrepreneurial advances, particularly in the financial service industry.

2.4.1 AMERICAN EMPLOYMENT PRACTICES

The indiscriminate layoff and hiring practices of American businesses may have been necessary to build the American economy and grow particular sectors in the past, but its current overuse has become questionable. Rather than for economic necessity, it is usually self-serving and covers up management failures or mistakes. Its overuse has a devastating effect on the public and on the American people in general. In fact, while it may temporarily solve or disguise a company's problems, it often has unexpected and sometimes disastrous effects on whole economic sectors.[5]

This hire-and-fire approach is also very expensive and largely ineffective. More often than not, it is used when management has run out of ideas to improve a company's competitiveness. Contrarily, these practices can result in declining competitiveness, less technological competence, and loss of worker morale and skill; in other words, the practice is often counterincentive. Furthermore, it usually results in loss of experience, group loyalty, and—even more importantly—loyalty to company, product, and process.

2.4.1.1 HOW AMERICA LOST ITS MANUFACTURING

America, which replaced England and Germany as the manufacturing and industrial giant earlier last century, lost its way in the last 30-40 years. While some of the blame lies with labor, which made outrageous financial and benefit demands; an equal share of blame lies with management, which became so self-righteous, self-important, top heavy, and incompetent that most American manufacturers lost their way. While claiming high productivity by American workers, even today, the reality is that their output is among the smallest multiples of their cost among developed countries.

True productivity is the ratio of value of total output divided by the cost of all inputs, and this is where American manufacturing is abysmally low. Not only will a Japanese or Korean shipbuilder construct an identical ship, car, or TV set with 40-60 percent of the man-hours required by an American manufacturer, but their white collar or overhead burden will be a fraction of that of their American counterparts. The argument used

---
5   Utohitelle, Louis, *The Disposable American*, Knopf, New York, 2006.

to be that American manufacturers had higher labor costs; yet today hourly labor costs in many countries in Europe and Japan exceed those in America, even after adding social costs. The difference is often that other overhead costs—those of excessive middle and upper management—are a multiple in America. This is not only because of excess numbers of people but also because of the unconscionably high remuneration paid, particularly to so-called upper management. It is difficult to understand why American automobile or other manufacturing executives earn 10-20 times as much as their Japanese and German counterparts working for an equally large, yet more successful company, particularly as living costs in those countries exceed those in the U.S.

Jobless and staying that way assures that America and Americans are neither ready nor capable of a radical change in their economic conditions, attitude, expectations, and standards. Our most important problem is—and has been for some time—self-indulgence and consumption. We produce not to meet other people's needs but primarily our own needs and desires. Our infrastructure is in shambles, our services largely deficient, and we consume vastly more than we produce. Our expectations, largely fed by our leaders, are unreasonable, unsustainable, and unjustifiable.

We were told for too long that consuming is good and that by consuming we will be able to correct our economy. Production output must equal or exceed consumption in the long run for sustainability. Output must be useful and in demand, otherwise it is useless. In recent years, Americans have increasingly enlarged the gap between consumption and production and in fact produced less and less useful, desirable, sellable goods and services.

America's economy is today largely self-serving and self-indulging. Although American products still dominate many world markets, U.S. content in appliances, cars, planes, and other manufactures has declined so much that in many cases they can no longer be termed American products. In many, only the intellectual concept, technology, or design is really American; and little of the actual manufactured good is made in America, independent of the mark or development of the good.

Even the intellectual content of manufactured goods requires less and less human input because electronic data and computer-aided design have replaced much of the need for human engineering and design inputs. Furthermore, many foreigners from large producing countries such as China, India, and Vietnam are educated in America;

yet, unlike in the past, they now often return to their home country to develop, design, and plan production of manufactured goods and large-scale infrastructure. Even macro projects in which America excelled in the past are now increasingly planned, designed, and executed abroad.

In other words, we have less and less to sell to pay for what we need, consume, and usually import. Many foreign firms are now beating us at our own game. One example is that of American designed and built warships that were sold to Korea with a proviso that they would get the designs and permits to build follow-up ships in Korea. Though lacking large naval vessel production experience, the Korean yard built top quality replica vessels in less time than the experienced U.S. yard.

2.4.2 Skewed Salary and Reward Systems

Salaries, bonuses, and other rewards are completely out of line in many sectors of the American economy, including finance, sports, and even academic institutions. In most countries, salaries and other rewards for senior management, professionals, or star levels used to be measured in terms of ratios to average rewards of professionals in that field. So, for example, CEOs of manufacturing companies would receive a reward (salary plus bonuses) of say 20 times that of a senior professional in their organization. Or, the CEO and chairman of Mitsui, one of the world's largest and most successful companies, would receive rewards amounting to $2 million dollars.

Compare this to the obscene reward packages in American financial institutions, some sports, and even private academic institutions. The latter has caught the prevalent greed fever, and some university presidents (Suffolk University in Boston as an example) reward themselves with salaries of 20-40 times those of experienced and renowned professors in their own organizations. Similarly, popular sports figures now demand salaries of $10-30 million, often 40-50 times those of average but competent players. As a result, many sport teams are now pricing themselves out of the market because ticket prices have risen at more than three times the rate of inflation, as have college costs at private institutions.

In addition, these rewarded stars often receive a variety of fringe benefits such as accommodations, official cars, use of private jets, and more. Many of these obscenely rewarded people spend their money on prestige investments or properties, and drive prices up as they compete with each other for prestige. This in turn has negative effects on the market and encourages merchants and developers to offer ludicrous or gross types of assets in housing, transport, and jewelry or other ornaments.

Luxury assets from properties to jewelry have, as a result, escalated in price at 4-6 times the rate of inflation, and their prices no longer bear any relation to their utility or even value. Most importantly, this has a severe adverse effect on the economy and on societal values. We increasingly reward failure, gambling, brinkmanship, and showmanship, not contribution.

In the long run, economies and societal stability require rational valuation of contributions and rewards measured in realistic terms of value to society. Fame should be rewarded by opening doors and allowing more rapid advance not by handing outrageous economic assets that in most cases are then wasted. In fact, one of the problems with the American economy is that so much of our investments are not in productive but rather in prestige assets. This is a huge waste and a major reason for our economic downturn, as we have too few productive assets.

2.4.3 Corruption in America

Americans are usually told and feel that we are the most honest and non-corrupt society. While we are certainly more honest than many people and countries, we are far from being an honest, non-corrupt society. Corruption in America is often more subtle, but it exists at most levels of society and government. It includes direct bribes or payments, self-serving favors, and allowing things to happen with a cover-up. This undermines American law enforcement and regulation as well as the basic concept of honest, law-abiding society.

Some of the largest corruption cases in human history occurred in the U.S. The Madoff pyramid scheme in which investors were defrauded of tens of billions of dollars tops the scale. It was largely possible because regulators who should have uncovered the scheme had a long history of close relationships and revolving door opportunities with the people and organizations they were supposed to regulate. But the SEC is not unique.

Similar problems exist in practically all areas of the economy. Increasingly, these lapses in enforcing regulations and laws endanger not only the economy but also health and safety in America. As a result, it is not surprising that many in the public are suspicious of government's role in financial, health care, food safety, and other regulations.

Corruption or conflict of interest is not only common among regulators, but is also common among politicians. No other country has or allows the degree of influence peddling called lobbying or even direct quid pro quo arrangements to influence lawmakers that America does. Direct and indirect influence peddling as well as trading is not only common but by now a well established procedure. It is not by chance that practically all representatives and senators who are supposed to represent all Americans are primarily lawyers. There are very few representatives of other professions who could throw effective light on important issues. Many other countries are largely guided and represented by technocrats who represent the whole array of activities and interests affected by laws and regulations under consideration. And it is also not by chance that most government officials come from and expect to return to the firms, companies, and organizations they are regulating, governing, or financing. No wonder that, as a result, they will often cooperate or coordinate decisions with them.

2.5 THE NEW AMERICAN UPPER CLASS

For a long time people were distinguished in socio-economic terms as belonging to the lower (poor), middle (reasonably well off), or upper (rich) class, with America definitely a largely middle-class nation. The American middle class included small businessmen, professionals, and the bulk of skilled and even lower-skilled workers. In fact, nearly 75 percent of Americans considered themselves to be middle class. Part of this was due to the American penchant for home ownership, which usually permitted people—even those of low income—to build up equity resulting in financial credibility.

In recent years, a new class has emerged; not one based on sweat-earned income or one of wealth creation from risk taking or innovative investments and developments, but from obscene and unscrupulous scams or other types of underhanded and often unconscionable schemes. This new class—which we will call the obscene wealth class—distinguishes itself by achieving their wealth at a young age and flaunting it without consideration for class, culture, or morality. They enjoy not the wealth and what it can buy but the show-off prestige they imagine is accruing to them.

Most of this class were failures in their educational aspirations and, as a result, resorted to a career of financial scams and show-off activities where obscene wealth exposure is the measure of success. Few if any in this new class ever contributed anything of value or permanency, and all they can usually show is social devastation left in the wake of their activities. But they are a proud bunch who try to outdo each other and are often supported by their employer or their own organization who themselves benefit from ever more unconscionable and often obscene schemes. These schemes and this wealth milk government and the trusting public; and they are negative as they only devalue real assets.

As I followed many graduate students' careers over the years, I was surprised to find a consistent pattern whereby the good and brilliant science and engineering students tended to have successful professional careers, became leaders in their fields, and were making contributions to science, technology, society, or culture. The others usually had big bank accounts, obscene show-off investments, and people as well as societal wealth in ruins; whereas the traditional wealthy or upper class generally contributed economic value and technological as well as systems or services improvements. This new class of Americans (usually in their thirties)—who could not succeed in anything but immoral, obscene schemes and endeavors—are now claiming a role in this country's economic, social, and political leadership, a trend which will hasten America's downfall as a world leader.

The "mis-contribution" of this new class is economically and politically highly destructive, as they completely distort the social value system; and this leads to a blurring of what is really valuable and what makes a great society. With few if any exceptions, they have neither culture nor conscience. They assume little if any responsibility for the damage they cause and the misery they leave behind and feel that their unconscionable show-off and obscene uncultured consumption is proof of success. They are the true cannibals of the 21st century.

2.5.1 American Immigration and Emigration

While many European and some Asian countries depended for long on immigrants for labor, North and South America attracted immigrants as settlers who would make their new country their permanent home, integrate into its society, and become its citizens. Attitudes towards immigration, the role of migrants, their rights and duties were and are as a result quite different. In European countries, they were either brought in to perform particular jobs or they came legally, and more often illegally, to improve their life and take advantage of opportunities including generous family support as well as other handouts. As a result, the latter were usually considered an unwelcome burden in many European countries, while until a few decades ago all types of immigrants were treated as welcome prospective citizens in the Americas, and particularly in the U.S.

Migrants play an increasingly important role in the world, because more people are on the move due to ease of travel, less difficult access, availability of information about possible destinations, human rights protections, and the globally more open economy. In America, nearly 28 percent of residents and 15 percent of citizens are foreign born; while in UK it's just fewer than 10 percent, in France about 16 percent, a similar number for Germany and Spain, and Italy falls somewhere in between. In Germany, many foreign workers were brought in largely from Turkey some decades ago, and many stayed and brought up families; while many immigrants in the UK, France, Spain, Italy, Holland, and Belgium, among others, came illegally and stayed, attracted by well developed social programs and support and higher living standards.

Comparatively, fewer came for a specific job or even to find a job, and many live on social benefits which are quite generous for families with a large number of children. While some assimilate well and successfully attempt to learn the language, customs, and ways of their new home country, there are many who neither care nor attempt to assimilate to their new environment, even if they bring up their children there.

Migrants can often be distinguished by their motives (usually economic), although there are now many other motives such as political, family reunion, education, and religious preference. In recent years, America has allowed in about one million per year: about half were sponsored by relatives; 320,000 entered temporarily; and about 0.5-1.0 million entered illegally. Many illegal immigrants reside in America temporarily so the actual annual population due to illegal immigrants is probably closer to half a million per year.

In addition, we have refugees and asylum seekers who try to escape persecution of various sorts and are usually admitted by Western countries, including America in large numbers. Actual numbers are hard to determine as many enter illegally and then apply for asylum, but the number admitted to the U.S. has fallen from 40-80,000/year in the 1980-90 period to probably no more than 20-30,000 per year now.

Altogether there may be as many as 200 million immigrants in the world-at-large. Migration traditionally has been from China, South and South Asia to Europe and America and from Africa to Europe. Many claim that much of the sustained economic growth, particularly in Europe, East Asia, and America has been fostered by decades of migration which fed the workforce, particularly in America. This has not only filled low skill jobs but also replenished young workers as more and more people in developed countries and particularly America retire early.

At the same time, migration often reprieves developing countries of important, often skilled and educated workers who seek greener pastures elsewhere, while developed countries export unskilled or lower skill work to poorer lower cost countries. While this had been the process in the 1980s and 1990s, the two major developing countries, China and India, have since developed more sophisticated economies with more attractive rewards and opportunities for skilled educated workers to retain or return them home, a strategy which certainly worked in China and is increasingly effective in India as well. These developments had severe effects on the American economy, at first on manufacturing and now more recently on high tech and other industries.

2.5.2 Economic Impact of Immigration

Over history rich countries have taken more skilled immigrants than ever before which, according to the World Bank has delayed and sometimes prevented the economic development of poor countries. At the same time, one could argue that many who emigrate to more developed countries such as America often improve their skills, education, and professional competence which, if they later return to their homeland, benefit its development. This is certainly true in China and now more recently India. In both countries much of the rapid economic and technological developments were driven or at least accelerated by large numbers of returning emigrants who attained new and advanced skills, particularly in America.

As an example which most Chinese graduate students at American universities looked for permanent careers in America in the past, nowadays many return to China after finishing their education and receiving some experience. This is a new and unaccustomed phenomenon for America which always assumed that immigrants would want to not only learn in America but become Americans with all its values. No more as significant students and immigrants return to their homeland not just for cultural, social or family reasons but because they perceive growingly attractive professional and economic opportunities in a more familiar and often attractive environment. This counter migration not only results in great losses for the American economy, but also develops increasingly potent economic, technological, trade, and even cultural competition.

America's immigration policy was been in tatters for decades now and attempts by Congress to fix it have failed repeatedly. The difficulty is that as a country of immigrants, there is a distinct distaste against regulation of immigration in general; yet a fairly universal feeling that something should be done to reduce illegal immigration and the entry of anti-American, criminal or potential terrorist elements. However, this is not only difficult but also counters the general liberal approach to immigration in America. Compared to most other countries, borders as well as internal movement control of foreigners in America are actually quite lax. There is no resident registration, hotels, and employers usually do not require personal identification and proof of legality. In other words, once a person is in the U.S., he or she is quite free to move about, work and engage in business or other activities with little change of being caught unless reported which is not very common.

This is quite different from the procedures adopted in many other countries where formal registration of residency, employment, and more with authorities is required. It is evident that America has not only lost much of its control over its borders with Mexico and Canada, but it has very scant control of people within its borders. True, as a preeminent democracy, we want as little interference by government in people's affairs, but at a time of international turmoil and rampant anti-Americanism in some quarters, the protection of America's values and people require more vigilance than we currently seem to exercise.

2.6 AMERICAN HEALTH CARE

America has developed a health care system that for many years and most of the 20th century was the envy of the world. It had a unique array of public and private hospitals and a huge effective and sophisticated health care and drug research system. It was at the forefront not only of medicine but also led in medical engineering, medical diagnostics, medical appliance development, and more. It also developed unique public/private cooperation in research, health care provision, drug development, and preventative including public medicine. Yet the very structure of the system encouraged many counter-incentive activities and actions.

Unique among nations, an adversarial and punitive system developed with lawyers chasing ambulances not to assure higher quality of reliable medical services, but to uncover minor and major deficiencies which could be used for demand of huge punitive damages, of which lawyers took a major part. In fact, unlike health care systems in other countries, the American health care system is burdened not only by the direct costs of malpractice and similar insurance, but also a huge amount of back up documentation and secondary evidential material.

Most of the paperwork burdening our health care system is imposed by the need for defensive measures to ward off potential liabilities and to meet the demands of insurers. In many other countries, these issues are all handled internally by medical and other boards of experts who are assigned powers of imposing disqualification, license revocation, as well as monetary penalties. This makes much more sense as in the end law courts and lawyers have to call in and rely on experts anyway.

The added cost of our legal requirements not only inflates our health care costs by 30-40%, but also results in the practice of defensive medicine or health care which has both short and long-term effects and certainly impacts on health care costs and quality. As a result of these factors, American health care, once the price of our nation, is now at about the same level as that provided in many developed and even some developing countries.

2.6.1 Improving the Quality and Cost of American Health Care

The year long Congressional debacle in 2009 on health care got off on the wrong foot and got buried in deeper and deeper mud. Instead of arguing ad infinitum about strategy and policy, we should have concentrated on just two issues and nothing else: (1) how to bring health care costs down and (2) how to improve American health care quality. Other issues such as health care accessibility or availability are so closely dependent and linked to these issues that starting at the other end as we did invariably had to lead to failure.

After spending the last two years in foreign and U.S. hospitals, it has become clear to me that our health care system is inefficient, self-serving, badly managed, and misused. Once we get our health care costs down, many of the other issues such as accessibility, quality, and affordability will solve themselves. There are many examples of high quality, low cost health care systems in the world and it is about time to learn from others instead of hiding behind the old excuse of "not made in America so it cannot be good or appropriate".

The quality and technology of the health care that I experienced in Malaysia, Israel, and other countries was vastly superior to that available here in America. Made in America is no longer an automatic sign of superior quality or even use of technology. Considering the major cost issues:

1. Legal Costs. Our tort system has distorted not only the quality and timeliness of our medical services, but adds at least 20% to their costs and causes use of defensive medicine. But defensive medicine causes other inefficiencies. Medical consent forms and reporting requirements in the U.S. are not only wasteful and counter-incentive but essentially useless. I never read nor could I possibly understand the fine print of consent forms I am asked to sign before a procedure, nor understand why my doctor had to spend twice as much time filling out records than the time it took for the procedure. Then there is the ambulance chasing and class action law practice which not only wastes time and money but contributes nothing to medical care except for costs. There is also the cost of administration of all these records. In fact, nearly half the administrative staff in our hospitals and doctors' offices would be redundant if these requirements were lifted. This does not mean or require elimination of medical record keeping or recording. Although much of modern information and communication technology was developed here, we lag far behind most other countries in its effective use in health care. Many foreign hospitals and other medical providers use electronic, remote reading record technologies with patients wearing electronic tags. Instead of fine print consent forms, they use verbal recorded consent agreements. Here the doctor (or other medical service provider) explains verbally what needs to be done and how it will be performed including potential hazards and side effects and asked the patient for verbal agreement to proceed. Patients have the opportunity to question and have their concerns answered before verbally agreeing to the procedure. These verbal agreements in most cases have the same validity as written (fine print) or signed agreements. Any claim of malpractice is adjudicated, not in a court of law, but before an arbitration panel of medical experts who are given the powers of courts of law. They not only have the power to revoke licenses but also impose fines and other penalties. This is much more efficient that a pure legal system which in the U.S. anyway requires medical experts to assist a court to render judgments. Medical records would be stored safely electronically. This way retrieving records would be easy and fast and require little human involvement. It also provides doctors with ready access to medical histories of patients and could cut hospital staff by 30-40%, while assuring greater accuracy and reliability and accessibility. These records would include not only procedural details but also medication, lifestyle data, and other information of use in providing quality, low cost health care.

2. The next issue is **health care marketing**. Here we, unlike most other advanced countries allow and even encourage advertising and marketing not just of medical services but also prescription medicines and treatments, something unheard of in most other countries. In fact some of the ads are outright misleading and presumptuous. It is really not a patient's job to tell the doctor what to prescribe. In addition some ads are really ridiculous. For example, the descriptions of side effects are usually misleading for lay persons. Marketing of drugs in the U.S. costs many times as much as anywhere else, a major reason why medications here are so much more expensive than elsewhere for the same medicine. The main difference is usually the cost of marketing. Drug marketing has also other costs which have little to do with education or information for doctors. All of this leads to exorbitant costs of drugs and medical supplies. Similarly, many hospitals and other health care providers spend a lot on marketing, even of devices paid for by government programs. If decisions for drugs and medical appliances were up to doctors alone, huge savings could be achieved in our health care systems

3. Medical Equipment and Technology Costs. Another major health care cost is the over-investment in and under-utilization of high cost medical diagnostic and remedial equipment. In many cases, there is duplication of expensive equipment by adjacent hospitals, with resulting under-utilization. Advanced medical equipment is often acquired not because of need but prestige with hospitals looking for effective use and-utilization often the investment is made. The same applies to medical specialists. Overall, there appears to be gross inefficiencies and wastes in our health care system which should be corrected before attempting a large-scale reorganization. It appears that 30-45% of our health care costs could be saved thereby bringing our health care in line with that of other advanced countries, with an improvement in the quality and accessibility of our health care system. As an example, an 800-bed, top quality hospital in most advanced countries employs about 1000 staff versus three to four times as many people in a typical American hospital of that size. The main difference is in administrative, accounting, public affairs, and similar duties, most of which are done perfunctorily. Counting aspirin tablets so they can be billed at $2/tablet is waste and contributes nothing to quality of health care. On a typical day in a hospital in the U.S., I counted over 20, most of whom performed narrow, simple tasks, such as changing towels. Considering U.S. health care costs, nearly half seem to contribute little if anything to actual health care. The main non-medical costs are malpractice insurance, maintenance of consent agreements, medical fine print documents mainly concerned with liability concerns, patient paper copies of personal details, treatments, and other information, duplication of expensive testing and other equipment, lack of electronic data storage and communication, drug advertising and marketing, hospital and medical service advertising and marketing. These and other costs such as class actions constitute over one-third or more of American health care costs and are the primary factors causing the high cost of health care in this country. Few if any of these costs or items contribute anything to American health care quality, availability or accessibility. In fact, in many areas of health care, the U.S. is far behind other countries which spend a fraction of what we spend on health care per patient. In addition, defensive medicine and lack of universal access to high-class health care to many causes American quality measures such as life expectancy as well as many treatments to lack those achieved in other countries.

2.6.2 Wellness Care

We have to change our emphasis on health care and put more weight on wellness care. Americans have access to some of the world's finest medical institutions, but are on average less healthy than people in other developed countries. Much of this is due to our life style, not just in terms of the food we consume, both quantity and quality, but also lack of effective exercise, unnecessary stress, unhealthy environment (air, water, etc.), and our over-emphasis with prestige.

We on average eat too much, worry too much, and do not relax effectively. As a result, not only is our life expectancy lower than possible, but our quality of life also suffers. Stress and lack of moderation are probably the major culprits, both of which are largely caused by our way of life, expectations, and socio/political environment.

We take ourselves too seriously and always insist on being first; this not in order to excel but to achieve the prestige of superiority. It is both amusing and disturbing that we always have to emphasize that we are tops or first. Be it in claiming that we are the best, biggest, most productive, finest or richest. In many cases, this makes no sense and only gives us a temporary, ill-conceived, unearned sense of well being and superiority.

In reality, our productivity, education, and even quality of health care lag behind that of many developed countries. In fact, we do have superior inventiveness and in many areas of technology provide incentives and opportunities that encourage some of our best and brightest to advance, invent, and develop, particularly in areas of technology. However, at the same time, these freedoms, lack of moral guidelines, and societal regulation have led us repeatedly into financial, political, and even educational abyss; this largely because of our over-confidence, misplaced optimism, lack of regulation, as well as moral guidance. We claim superiority in many fields where we actually lag behind not only the best but even world averages.

The traditional pay for service health care reimbursement system is counter-incentive, both in terms of health care quality and cost. Recently Blue Cross and Blue Shield of Massachusetts proposed paying doctors and hospitals a flat sum per patient each year plus a large bonus if they improve care. This would have the providers working more closely together, cooperating, and assuring quality. The idea is to increase the empowerment of providers and assure closer cooperation as well as responsiveness to patients.

Although Americans pay more for health care in real and relative terms than any other people in the world, we have higher infant mortality and rates of preventable deaths than any other industrialized country. Our health care system is quite inefficient, over-manned and at the same time under-staffed, wasteful and in many cases unresponsive to the public's needs. It is burdened by very complex organizational structures, an unnecessary complex bureaucracy and a lot of conflicting interests. It is burdened by complex legal and so-called malpractice safeguards which do little if anything to improve the quality and/or safety of health care but burdens the system with inefficient and largely self-serving bureaucracy and administration.

Our health care system has the highest overhead and a larger percentage of costs are spent on non-health care related services than in any other country in the world. A typical quality hospital in the U.S. has 2-3 times the staff as an equally large service and quality hospital in any other country. The amount of paperwork and administrative staff required is usually a multiple of that abroad.

We reward disease treatment but spent little on disease prevention. Many medical decisions are made based on their economics, not on the best medical practice. Our main problems are that we do not emphasize prevention enough and when illness or injury occurs are often led towards the most profitable not beneficial procedures. This applies to diagnostic and medical procedures. The excessive use of x-rays, MRIs, cat scans, etc. is largely driven by economic and not health care interest. Similarly, information management is usually performed by hand and not use of the most advanced electronic technology; this notwithstanding the fact that most advanced medical information, testing, and diagnostic technology originated in America. The reasons appear to be largely tort related.

2.6.3 AMERICA'S DRUG PROBLEM

America is the world's largest consumer of drugs notwithstanding severe penalties and drug enforcement laws. In fact, nearly 30% of prisoners in American jails are incarcerated for drug-related offenses. The vast majority of these is either first time offenders or incarcerated for minor drug-related crimes. The cost of this is in the hundreds of billions, yet few if any of those incarcerated for minor drug-related crimes get effective rehabilitation treatment. As a result, a significant percentage becomes repeat offenders.

These prisoners are on the whole not violent and could or should perform meaningful work as part of their rehabilitation. In other words, our drug prevention laws damage society in several ways.

1. They do not effectively treat drug users.
2. They impose the cost of incarceration on the public.
3. They prevent even minor drug offenders from performing meaningful work or otherwise contribute to society.
4. They contribute to the potential of making a first or initial drug user into a habitual drug user.
5. They increase the dependence of first time or non-habitual drug users on drug dealers and pushers.

Other countries are dealing with the drug problem much more effectively by decriminalizing first time and minor drug use and by providing more effective control of the drug trade. In other words, they severely punish drug traders and pushers, particularly those involved in selling drugs to minors or in an organized fashion.

They similarly use media and public opinion to dissocialize drug use, the way it was done with alcohol, cigarettes (tobacco), and more in this country. There is too little public information on the debilitating effects of drugs on sex, social relations, brain functions, and ability to perform. Drug use must be made socially unacceptable and with new efficient social networks there are real opportunities to push the point and make drug users/pushers social outcasts.

It has become evident that the problem is really driven by American demand for drugs and that we must finally face the fact that unless demand is curbed by strict punishment of users and strict legal control of distribution, we will never solve the drug problem. Just going after the suppliers, drug dealers, smugglers, etc. just cannot work. It never did and never will. History has shown that demands will always be met, particularly if supported by a willingness to pay whatever it takes. This is true for drugs, sex, and everything else human's desire intensely or to which they are addicted. Let us finally get real and attack the roots of the problem even if solutions are politically difficult or unpopular. We owe it to the country, our children, and generations to come.

America has the world's biggest drug problem not only because it consumes more drugs than anyone else but also because it is unwilling to control the drug trade forcefully. While most Western countries have strict laws dealing with drug sales as well as consumption, America goes mainly after the drug dealers. It is interesting to note that drug consumption is mainly by the middle class, it increasingly also involves students and even children in both rich and poor neighborhoods. There are Western countries in South East Asia such as Singapore which introduced draconian disincentives such as the death penalty for both dealers and consumers in possession above a certain amount.

At this time, it is interesting to note that drug addiction is quite low in many drug producing countries such as Burma, Afghanistan, Bolivia, Colombia, and more. This in part is due to religious objection which prohibits consumption of intoxicating drinks as well as the consumption of drugs. Religious rules seem to greatly affect drug consumption and trading.

There are insignificant drug problems among devout Muslims and Jews, among others. Although China had a serious opium addiction period, all together drug addiction overall is well under control, this particularly among devout or culturally actives. Somehow most Orientals find other recreations more relaxing and satisfying.

America will have to radically change its drug interception approach and go not only after the dealers but also the users. As long as there is significant demand, the drug business will thrive and involve more and more of American society.

Drugs not only have become a major health issue and cost in America, but contribute greatly to national crime, border insecurity, and delinquency. In fact, the cost of the impact of drugs on the national economy have been estimated to exceed 10% of GDP, of which about one third are each the cost of added health care, law enforcement, and loss of productive output. In addition, there are the costs of homeland insecurity, border control, and more.

For many years we have tried to reduce or solve this problem by intercepting the supply, with little success. In fact, drug smugglers have come up with ever more imaginative ways to import and distribute drugs. One of the latest means used are semi- or full submersibles which can carry tons of cocaine, etc., practically undetected and largely undetectable across the Gulf of Mexico and/or the West Coast. It is increasingly evident that the U.S. drug problem will not be solved by interdiction, border control, and law enforcement, but very much like other problems caused by addiction.

We must solve this problem at home. As long as there is high demand backed by large amounts of money, someone will find a way to meet the demand. The time has come to start to criminalize drug use as well as drug trading; this in parallel with strictly controlled, prescriptive use of drugs for well-defined medical purposes would go a long way in drastically reducing the market price and value of drugs. We must aggressively reduce drug use and demand. The cost of demand control enforcement will be significantly lower than the cost of drug law enforcement as done today.

It has become evident that the problem is really driven by American demand for drugs and that we must finally face the fact that unless demand is curbed by strict punishment of users and strict legal control of distribution, we will never solve the drug problem. Just going after the suppliers, drug dealers, smugglers, etc. just cannot work. It never did and never will. History has shown that demands will always be met particularly if supported by a willingness to pay whatever it takes. This is true for drugs, sex, and everything else humans desire intensely or to which they are addicted. Let us finally get real and attack the roots of the problem even if solutions are politically difficult or unpopular. We owe it to the country, our children, and generations to come.

2.6.4 Curbing National Obesity

Physical obesity of Americans has been in the limelight for some time and recognized as a major health problem and cause for spiraling health costs in the U.S. However over-consumption of goods, supplies, and other services is equally if not more rampant and poses a huge economic, social, and cultural threat to America. It is well know that we consume significantly more fuel, clothing, building materials, water, and other goods than any other people on a per capita basis. As a result, we also generate significantly more waste and demand much more services just to take care of our waste.

Most Americans have a huge number of things including toys, clothing, and tools, appliances that they never or seldom use and bought on an impulse or under marketing pressure. The same applies to services which Americans consume or buy if they need them or not. The problem is that most services impose significant public expenditure. Waste disposal costs in the U.S. are a multiple of those in equally advanced countries such as Europe, Japan, etc.; legal services impose court, police, and other law enforcement agency costs which are not paid by the litigant or his law firm but by the public. Similarly, while many pay for waste removal, disposal and recycling costs including the environmental impacts are usually borne by the public at large.

Americans have developed a culture of superiority. They are constantly told that they are the best, richest, most educated, and have the highest standard of living. Though much of this may have been true 40 years ago, its educational standards are mediocre, even its health care and other institutions are increasingly falling behind those of other nations. While America still maintains the world's largest and probably most powerful military, it is no longer preeminent in many areas of science and technology which today affects military eminence.

At the same time, the country is falling increasingly into more debt, greater dependence, and mediocrity in education, science, technology and more. If America is to retain or regain its eminence as a leading nation, it will have to take drastic actions, some of which may be politically and economically painful, yet necessary. The most important is to recognize that America is no longer the richest, best, and most advanced country or society.

Next is to learn not only to live within our means but consume no more than we produce or the value of our output justifies. While most recognize that a zero sum game governs all long term systems, nations, family or other units, we have for long consumed out of all proportion to our output or even legitimate needs. In other words, we have been over-eating just because the food was there, cheap, and being offered. The same applied to other things.

Americans change appliances, cars, etc. not when they are old, worn out or too expensive to use, but because they always want the latest, the most advanced, etc., not necessarily because they need it or even know how to use it, but because others have it. In other words, independent of need or usefulness, Americans buy stuff just because someone else did.

The same applies to services and therefore there are usually avalanches of legal or other developments not because of real or legitimate grievances but because it has become fashionable and others succeeded with such demands, justified or not. There is an urgent need to reduce consumption to what people need or want to use. The 'me too' and artificially generated demands, most of which play on people's vanity, ambition or fear, must be changed.

Most advanced Western countries do this by imposing a meaningful consumption tax (VAT, etc.) of 15-20%; this not only curtails consumption but also offers significant, fairly distributed revenues to government. Such a tax should also be applied to most services, such as legal services and consulting. Only this way will use be able to not just reign in unnecessary and frivolous consumption but also reimburse the taxpayers or public for the extra public costs imposed such as court costs, policing, waste disposal, etc.

As a people, we only want to win. We agree to reward Wall Street dealers when they win when gambling with their client's money but not to lose or pay a penalty when they lose in playing with their client's money. Similarly, lawyers chase ambulances to identify potential clients for malpractice suits, they can only win, not lose, and nobody but taxpayers pays for the cost of courts, etc. used in that procedure. In many other countries, malpractice and similar claims are investigated and adjudicated by boards of professionals (doctors, engineers, etc.) who have the professional knowledge to judge malpractice and the power to withdraw professional licenses as well as impose other penalties. Yet claimants and their lawyers have to pay the cost of arbitration, including the cost of any impartial investigations or tests required by the judges. The public is not charged for the costs of claim adjudication.

Such an approach is not only more fair, timely, and just, but also saves public money and time as the claimants have greater control over the timing of the arbitration board hearings.

2.6.5 The Future of U.S. Health Care

American health care has finally become universal, thanks to the Obama administration health care bill which assures coverage for all Americans and also improves many of the details of health care access and delivery. It fails to a large extent in addressing many of the inefficiencies of our health care system, most importantly the malpractice insurance and similar legal hurdles which make the system a bonanza for the legal profession and insurance industry without materially improving either the quality or accessibility of U.S. health care. In fact, as pointed out before it introduces major hurdles by imposing not only huge additional costs, but also often life threatening delays in the health care delivery. Most other advanced countries leave such decisions to experts and not legal practitioners.

One of the reasons for much of the inefficiencies in our health care system is the need for hard copy documentation which wastes physician, patient, and nurses' time, yet introduces little if any improvements in quality of medical services. It did also delay the introduction of electronic data and information systems which were not only developed in the U.S., but are readily available and generally used by our military and most foreign hospitals. Patients seldom are able or willing to read and understand the various so-called consent documents they are required to sign to obtain a medical procedure.

The cost in time and operations or facilities to maintain all these records absorbs a significant percentage of our health care costs and causes unnecessary delays in delivery, without improving care. All it does is legally protects practitioners from frivolous law suits by ambulance chasers who seldom have patient well being in mind. In fact, the time has come, in my opinion, to get lawyers out of health care, with the exception of evident criminal behavior or behavior with malice by medical providers. Lawyers and insurers should concentrate on prevention of criminal types of activities, including criminal conduct.

In parallel, we probably need a reevaluation of the use of technology and greater coordination in the use and sharing of technology by hospitals and diagnostic service providers. Increasingly hospitals and other health care providers push certain services to improve utilization of equipment, facilities, and services whether needed or not. In other words, many procedures and services are now driven by economic or financial (including profit) considerations instead of being purely based on medical and patients' health care interests.

Marketing of drugs and pharmaceutical products is similarly increasingly driven by profit and not quality and medical or health issues, with some of the advertising not just misleading. In fact, advertising of prescription drugs should be discouraged as patients should not be involved in or encouraged to advise their doctor what drug to prescribe. Some of the drug advertising is also misleading or outright counter incentive. For example, warnings that side effects of a drug may be life-threatening and suggesting if that occurs, patients should call their doctor right away. The ad does not suggest how a comatose or deceased patient would be able to contact his or her doctor. The money spent on such misleading or outrageous ads would be better spent on improving drugs or reducing the often outrageous cost of drugs.

America needs to do more to encourage healthy lifestyles by encouraging healthy eating, reasonable food quantities, smoking cessation, and breathing polluted air. We could reduce our outrageous health care costs by 40-50% and increase life expectancy and well being if we could

- Get the lawyers out of health care
- Improve health care facility and service efficiency and capacity utilization
- Improve American's life style, particularly by reducing obesity, smoking, and over-sizing meals and portions
- Assure people become physically more active
- Make health care, medication, and sport facilities more accessible and affordable
- Stop general drug marketing and replace it by general health care information, including specific suggestions of improving eating, life style, exercise, and interpersonal relations and communications.

Most importantly, more effective information must be made available and incentive provided, particularly to the young to develop and enjoy a healthier life style.

Americans are great sport lovers, but as they grow older are mainly sport observers and not participants. This trend starts in school which emphasizes, encourages, and invests in prestige sports, such as American football which only few can and will play and which requires outrageously expensive facilities and equipments. At the same time, participatory sports such as soccer, athletics, and more are discouraged. As a result, few students actually participate and benefit from the large and expensive sports programs. Winning and prestige are good, but ultimately only sports which allow all to participate and improve their health really count and fulfill the promise.

In the U.S. health care has finally become a right instead of a privilege during 2009 when the Obama administration was able to pass new health care laws which made health care universally accessible and affordable. No longer are the uninsured required to burden emergency rooms in hospitals with their ills and general health care becomes the norm. In the U.S. health care is expected to also become much more efficient; this largely with the introduction of modern information and information management systems, and hopefully reduction of the malpractice prevention mismanagement which requires a huge bureaucracy, inordinate paperwork and records keeping, all of which makes no sense in this electronic age.

In fact, studies indicate that if the legal process in U.S. health care were handled by professional arbitration panels instead of lawyers and the courts not only would the quality of health care in the U.S. improve and its costs go down but it would also become much more responsive to health care needs. New diagnostic technology which permits, for example, blood pressure, pulse, and ECG be measured by a cell phone-type device and results directly transmitted to a physician should permit a large reduction not only of provider's time but also improve both accessibility and health control at a huge reduction in costs.

2.7   AMERICA'S INFRASTRUCTURE MANAGEMENT
Since large-scale rebuilding of America's infrastructure, particularly interstate highways nearly 60 years ago under President Eisenhower which both vastly improved America's highways and logistics systems and generated huge amounts of work (jobs) as well as large-scale purchase

of materials and equipment, very little large-scale infrastructure investment has been made in the U.S. Since that time, America's road, water, sewage, electric distribution, and rail infrastructure has become highly deficient and is now in a very dilapidated state.

In parallel, even state and local road, sewage, water, electric, and gas infrastructure are in pretty bad shape, ill-maintained, and often quite antiquated. Compared to Europe and even East Asian infrastructure (China, Japan, Korea, etc.), America is now well behind, not only in the lack of high-speed trains and modern, efficient airports, but also in ports and even basic mundane infrastructure such as local electric power, telephone, gas, sewage, and other distributed systems.

We are the only modern, developed country in the world where many distributed systems are hanging from wooden poles and underground water and gas pipelines are buried and hard to inspect or maintain. The failure of the levees in New Orleans during the Katrina hurricane disaster was the result of lack of maintenance and repair and not failures of design and construction. Recent studies indicate that the cost of repair and downtime of wires ruptured by ice and snow in winter in New England, for example, would easily pay for the cost of putting all these wires underground.

However the problem is more far-reaching. A major issue as in other areas of the U.S. economy is the lack of clear identification of responsibility and control. While in many countries government takes a leading role in infrastructure development, financing, control/management, and maintenance, there is no clear demarcation of such responsibility in America. However, private industry has maximizing profit and minimizing cost as its prime objectives and therefore objects to restrictive rules and conditions. As a result, infrastructure developments as well as maintenance decisions are often driven more by profitability than public interest as well as safety. While in the short run this strategy may offer economic advantages, it lacks strategic focus and in terms of public economic benefits is highly deficient. At the same time notwithstanding advances in equipment, material, and building technology, productivity in infrastructure construction, repair, and maintenance has declined significantly, driving up costs and time, particularly downtime of essential infrastructure such as electricity, water supply, roads, rail lines, and more.

For example, while we were able to build the New York Empire State Building, the world's tallest building at the time, in just over a year 70-

80 years ago, it would take us more than twice the time and man-hours today notwithstanding the availability of more and advanced building equipment, material, and prefabrication.

2.7.1 Managing Large Projects and Disasters

For a long time America has enjoyed a reputation for effective managing large or macro projects; this mainly because America developed large infrastructure and other projects efficiently. These included the interstate highway system, Tennessee Valley Authority, Panama Canal, and more. The Empire State Building, for example, was built in just over one year. Similarly, the U.S. developed mass production of cars in Detroit and later ships in places like Hingham, Massachusetts where a Kaiser-led shipyard built 10,000 ton cargo ships in a few months. In fact, America built more ships in four years of World War II than in all U.S. shipyards during their history.

In more recent years, America's large project management capability suffered severe declines and it is doubtful that we could replicate these past successes even with today's massive new technological and equipment capabilities. Most importantly, America seems to have lost much of its emergency and disaster response management capability as evidenced by the Katrina and BP oil spill disasters.

In both cases, response was not only slow but in many ways ineffective and slow, this notwithstanding the availability of modern communication, transport, and engineering technology and equipment. There appears to be an increased amount of disconnect and lack of cooperation as well as coordination and effective management, this notwithstanding the fact that the U.S. is a leader in management schooling and systems development.

The major reasons for this disconnect appears to be lack of effective coordination and interacting or conflicting interests. This is most evident in management by government agencies or problems on projects for which government takes responsibility or leadership be they civil, military or logistics.

2.7.2 Hanging Wires, Cables, and Pipes

One major problem with American infrastructure, particularly with distributed systems such as electric power, telephone, etc. is that in most parts of the country these systems are not only very old and often ill maintained, but many of them are supported by poles and are not underground. As a result and particularly in the northern part of the country, there are major disruptions when in winter storms ice accumulation results in broken wires as well as poles. These in turn can cause serious and often expensive disruption, dangerous conditions as well as major expenses both public and private.

In fact in many communities the cost of damage and service disruptions would easily pay for putting these services permanently below ground. A large gas pipe explosion in San Bruno (California) in September 2010 showed ill-maintained, old pipelines can be a major hazard to life and property. In fact, most American urban infrastructure is more than 50 years old and not only often ill-maintained but not even regularly inspected. As a result, we suffer under numerous pipes and other distributed infrastructure failures endangering public safety and disrupting the economy and people's lives. We need a much more effective infrastructure and infrastructure testing and maintenance system.

American infrastructure development and maintenance has fallen in quality and efficiency. For example, the Empire State Building was completed in just over a year, with low capacity, antiquated machinery and tools. Today 80-90 years larger, we could not possibly build it in that time. Similar infrastructure building, repair, and improvements take many times as long as in most other countries. This is not only due to complex planning and approval processes and politics, but also largely due to low productivity, bad planning, and management as well as short sighted misplaced approaches. For example, small road repairs are usually done during rush hours and not only cause large traffic jams, but also huge added costs for police to divert traffic. Such and most infrastructure can and should be done in off hours. Improvements in efficiency would easily pay for the extra costs of over or night time work. Another issue is the waste of having millions of dollars worth of construction equipment sit idle for weeks, months, and sometimes years when jobs are started before all approvals and financing are in place. Some simple repair jobs which should take hours take weeks or months for no reason except incompetent planning, inefficiency, and often management and planning incompetence. In addition, obviously all of these factors inconvenience the public and otherwise affect our economy. While projects may not pay directly for traffic jams and added air pollution by idling cars, the overall economy of this nation is affected by it.

Another issue is the lack of or incompetent approach to inspection and basic maintenance. Rusty bridge steel work, washed out levees, and rotting dams or embankments as well as rotting power poles are among many deficiencies affecting our infrastructure. However, infrastructure is the life blood of an economy and while we were ahead of most nations in infrastructure availability and quality during much of the 20th century, this is no longer so. In fact, the quality, accessibility and capacity of our infrastructure is now well behind that of most developed and some developing countries.

2.7.3 America's Response Preparedness

Americans' used to be known as the can-do people and America has a nation capable of tackling any project however large and complex. From mass-producing thousands of large ships during World War II to building the Empire State Building in just about a year nearly one hundred years ago, America always proved itself up to the task, however complex or large. When JFK undertook for America to reach the moon with a life landing to respond to Russia's space advances in the early nineteen sixties to the construction of the Panama Canal, the Hoover Dam, and other great projects, America always proved itself up to the task and not only achieved great results but exceeded all expectations.

This can-do and self-confident approach to macro achievements, the envy of much of the world seems to be lost. In recent years America not only failed to respond to challenges and disasters effectively but often disappointed friend and foe alike with its response to major challenges, both manmade and natural. America was recently involved in three major disasters, the Katrina hurricane which hit southern Louisiana, primarily the New Orleans area, the Haiti earthquake, and the BP oil spill (Deepwater rig Horizon explosion).

Each of these was a major disaster and an opportunity for America to show its ability to respond effectively to disasters or emergencies. America failed in all three, showing not only an inability to effectively organize and respond to emergencies or disasters, but also to use its enormous resources to bear on large problems. In all three and other cases, the resources were there ready to be used, but the government and American organizations mismanaged the situation, missed opportunities or misused resources. In this report, we will review the actions taken, results missed or achieved and the causes for any failure or lack of effective response.

The two major disasters which hit the U.S. in 2005 and 2010 are typical examples of failure in response, commitment, and organization. In both cases, the problem and effects were not only evident but there was national support for determined action. Yet lack of effective organization, management, and ultimate execution led not only to a much larger than necessary and expected costs in physical, human, and economic terms, but also in terms of America's reputation as a can-do and committed responsible nation. It is uncertain how much a role politics and even conflicts of interests played in delaying and executing actions which in both cases resulted in greater than necessary damage and loss.

2.7.4 U.S. Mail Service Dilemma

Junk mail is not only clogging up the American postal system wasting large amounts of paper and causing huge added costs which are then dumped on the legitimate postal service users, largely letter users, but it has also degenerated into an often deceptive marketing ploy which invades private homes and gets people to buy things they neither need nor understand. As a result, the U.S. Postal Service is losing some of the most lucrative businesses to FedEx, UPS, and other private delivery services. This has nothing to do with freedom of expression, but is a direct invasion of privacy and misuse of public service. In addition, it causes a huge waste of resources, not just paper but also logistic service (trucking, mail delivery carting), and more.

There are better and cheaper ways to market goods and inform the public. In my normal household, we discard about 90% of all mailings without even opening them. Junk mail accounts for nearly 50% of waste paper in most households and its costs are many times the direct and indirect benefits to society. The problem is becoming proportionally worse with increased use of electronic mail and a consequent reduction in first class mail.

In fact, the proportion of junk mail has increased rapidly and has grown from 30-40% twenty years ago to over 80% now, yet its contribution to the costs of mail delivery has actually declined. It is estimated that this problem, both of waste and fairness, can only be solved by increasing the costs of junk mail service by at least 50% and brings it more in line to its costs and competing marketing methods, and junk mail charges in other countries. With residences in several countries (Europe, Middle East, and Far East), I can confirm that the junk mail problem is unique to the U.S. It causes not only a major financial burden but also environmental damage on society.

Junk mail provides little if any social benefit in terms of information or otherwise. As a result, society is burdened by a cost in monetary, environmental, and service terms out of all proportion to any benefit. To market goods and services, various other non-hard copy mailing methods are readily available such as the Internet, TV, and more which do not burden the public purse or environment. Bringing junk mailing charges in line with costs is expected to save taxpayers hundreds of millions and assure more effective mail service and delivery. It would similarly help the environment by reducing paper consumption and disposal again saving hundreds of millions of dollars.

The USPS lost $8.2b in 2009, mostly in the handling of junk mail. With the availability of the Internet, there is less and less justification for mass mailing marketing which, as noted, only ends up as waste paper without ever being noticed. As third class mail gets the same treatment and requires the same services as so-called first class mail, it should be charged the same. This would not only greatly reduce waste in paper, transportation, and administration, but also help the USPS to finally cover its costs and improve service.

The U.S. Postal Service is losing a lot of business due to the availability of electronic transactions such as electronic bill paying. As a result, it may have to provide other services or get involved in new businesses to cover its costs.

2.7.5 American Incompetence and Arrogance or Mismanagement of Disasters

The management of and response to the horrendous BP oil spill in the Gulf of Mexico is the most recent example of America's inability to deal with large problems. The reasons for the lack of effective response are many but all show that although we have the technology and resources to deal with large problems and disasters, our government and management structure prevent us from effective and timely responses to unforeseen disasters. Not only did the government fail to respond, but it also failed to use its legal powers to manage the response to this disaster.

This is not an Exxon Valdez or even a Katrina type and magnitude disaster but one of Chernobyl size and long term impact. The oil and chemicals used to break it up and disperse it from the visible to the ocean bottom will affect our Gulf beaches and marshes for decades, without any help for effective cleanup or remediation. There is a high probability that the effect of the leak (of at least 40,000 bls/day) will largely sink to below the surface and move or be moved by ocean currents to ultimately (later this year) enter the Gulf stream and pollute Cuba's, Florida's, and Bahama's and East Coast beaches and marshes. It may also pollute the beaches of Jamaica.

Although the U.S. government is holding BP responsible for the costs of the clean up, they are protected by a limitation clause which currently exposes them and their insurers to $75m. As a result, foreign countries damaged by this accident are going to blame and later sue us, America, for the damage and the international court will side with them and make us responsible for the cost of cleanup, loss of business/opportunity, and other damage. There are no limitations to awards or other costs.

Under international law, we, the U.S., are responsible for any economic damage caused to a neighboring country by anyone acting under our supervision and direction. The amazing fact is that while accidents can happen, it is necessary to take all precautions particularly when operating in unchartered waters or physical conditions never experienced. To use short cuts, ignore damage signs, and fail to provide all safety measures is criminal. The criminality is not just by the operator who has an economic goal but also or even more so by the regulators, inspectors, and licensors who were paid to supervise and control the project.

As we belatedly found out, the MMS which supervised the project, failed in the outrageous and probably criminal terms to fulfill its obligations. But the buck does not stop there; once the accident happened, the government all the way to the President made pious pronouncements that they will not only keep BP "responsible" (whatever that means) but also mobilize the full capability and resources of the government and America to deal with this monumental catastrophe.

Many like me and my colleagues, all experts in ocean and offshore sciences and engineering, expected to be called or mobilized to help devise and implement remedial actions; we not only waited but much like me bombarded the White House, administration, and Congress with offers, ideas, and solutions. Not only were they all ignored but the responsibility for dealing with all aspects of this calamity were given or transferred to BP, with minimal supervision or even oversight by the government.

The argument was that the knowledge and resources required to deal with this accident rested with or within BP not the larger oil industry, our National Science Foundation or institutes, world class ocean research institutes, universities, and industrial firms. It was as if to solve a crime we would hire the criminal to solve the crime as obviously the criminal knew where it was committed, by whom, and how. He was therefore uniquely qualified to solve the crime. Well BP's objectives and incentives were to minimize their faults, reduce the evidence of damage and downplay any potential effects. In other words, to hide not just the magnitude of the spill and malfeasance which caused it, but also hide the evidence by dumping enormous quantities of poisonous dispersants to make the oil disperse and/or sink below the ocean's surface.

Instead of this, they could have as was done in the case of a large spill in Saudi waters, mobilized large numbers of super tankers and pumped the concentrated oily water into these huge (1-3 million bls) tankers for later separation of the oil from the water. But this would have exposed them to the real quantity of oil leaking from the broken well. Hence they continued to insist on the use of huge quantities of dispersants and other chemicals, which would not only hide much of the evidence, but also damage beaches and marshes more and make it more difficult to clean up the ocean and coastlines.

As an experienced Ocean Engineer and author of the book on "Ocean Environmental Management"[6], I am disturbed and surprised at the lack of oversight and use of neutral American experts. As this well at 5,000 ft charted new territory, it should have been incumbent upon BP to not only introduce additional safeguards such as a second blow out preventer, but also used better submarine inspection. There are deep diving, manned submarines available that are equipped with robotic arms to manipulate mechanical devices, inspect, and control ocean bottom equipments, such as Woods Hole Oceanographic Institute's Alvin which could and should have been mobilized and prepositioned at the site to make sure everything is working well and be available to make corrections/adjustments if and when required. Instead work continued even after various defects and malfunctions occurred.

In addition, for very little BP could have mobilized a fleet of large tankers and skimmers to stand by just in case. In fact, it is inexcusable

---

6   Prentice Hall, New York, 1989.

that no fleet of super tankers which were readily available close by in the market, were mobilized after the accident to collect huge quantities of oily water accumulating at the site. The oily water could have been scooped up by these monstrously large tankers for transport to refineries or holding ponds for extraction of the oil. Chartering of a large tanker would have cost $40-70,000/day, much of which would have been recouped from the sale of the extracted oil. But this was never done.

This approach was used in numerous other bottom blowouts. Most recently at an offshore oil well failure in Saudi Arabia when large tankers and skimmers were used to remove much of the oily water from the site of the leak and prevent its accumulation and soiling of beaches as well as the open seas. Notwithstanding America's great wealth and institutions, it has shown itself shamefully inept in dealing with great disasters in terms of protection, response, and rebuilding. This has been shown repeatedly during great storms in Florida, the Katrina hurricane, the BP oil spill, various mining disasters, and more.

2.8 AMERICA'S EDUCATION SYSTEM

Just a few years after the criminal sub-prime mortgage disaster hit America's and later the global economy with a vengeance, we are at the threshold of a new and possibly bigger economic disaster also caused by greed, lack of oversight and regulation or government incompetence. While the sub-prime mortgage crisis enveloped the U.S. and later global financial institutions as well as American society, the new sub-prime student (educational) loan crisis will have much wider complications and last much longer. The sub-prime mortgage crisis affected banks and markets as well as people who lost their dwellings. The education crisis will affect society at large and many social institutions, the government, and society itself.

It will accelerate the lack of fiscal viability and possibly cause the insolvency of Social Security and other social support programs. It will also drive the U.S. economy further into debt with no chance of reversal, and it will make the debtor 'America' more dependent on other countries. Most importantly, it will undermine social standards and confidence.

America used to have one of the world's best education systems, both at the primary/secondary and tertiary (college, trade, university) levels, with some of the best research universities. While some of these are still at the forefront, the system in general has declined or deteriorated at all levels. Even more importantly, it has lost much of its focus. As noted, America spends more on education in both real and relative terms than any other country in the world, yet its standards have continuously declined in student performance and we now barely achieve the levels of students in some poor developing countries, particularly in math and science.

Although the federal government supports education in general, basic school funding at the primary and secondary levels is usually local. As noted, as a result poor communities automatically spend significantly less per student than affluent ones. This ratio may be as large as 3 to 1. However, poor communities actually need better and more supportive school systems as children get less home and community support. Furthermore, they need more extended school hours, facilities for after class, homework, and supervision as fewer children of poor families are assured of support and supervision at home after school. They may also lack a quiet environment and basic furnishings to support after school study.

It is becoming increasingly evident that American education needs a radical change and renewal. Our educational system is the most expensive in the world, yet our performance or the grades our students achieve have been falling for decades and are now lower than those of equivalent students in many poor developing countries. Much of this has to do with the way education is organized, funded, and regulated in this country. The end results though are that

1. We spend more money or percentage of our economy (GDP) than any other country in the world, yet many schools are failing, dilapidated, and employ often unqualified and/or unmotivated teachers who receive tenure and are protected by powerful national unions.
2. Students in America spend significantly more years in school than in most countries, yet more often than not graduate without marketable or usable knowledge or skills. In America more than 82% of high school leavers continue on to college or tertiary education to spend another three or four years largely to learn what they could and should have learned in high school. The vast majority of high school leavers enter liberal arts colleges which are really remedial high schools.
3. Because we teach what students and teachers want, not what

is needed to satisfy the needs of society and our economy including education and focus on skills needed to fill real productive job opportunities and other needs, many of our graduates are unable to find jobs after graduation at age 22 and have to spend another 2-4 years learning a profession or marketable skill. While this is fine for talented and motivated youth, there are many who even after college, usually a liberal arts school where all they did was, as noted, learn what they should have learned in high school, still do not know what they want and where to acquire the knowledge and skills required for a meaningful job and career.

4. As a result, students in the U.S. usually enter the productive work force 3-4 years later than in most other countries and even then often lack the motivation, skills, and knowledge to perform. With 83% of all high school leavers in the U.S. continuing to tertiary (college) education and nearly two-thirds of those opting for or being admitted by liberal arts programs and colleges which is over twice the percentage of tertiary school attendees in other countries such as the UK, France, Germany, Japan, and more, while China allows a dismal 17% to continue to college. While these percentages may be fine for a small service-oriented economy, this is counterproductive and counterincentive in the world's largest economy with 5% of the world's population. But the implications for the American economy are huge. With nearly all young people starting meaningful work only at the age of nearly 22 years instead of 18.5 as in most other countries and a retirement age of 65, people in general lose about 4 years of productive or about 10% of or total working life of 40 years. This means a greatly reduced life income, income tax, and Social Security contributions, as well as huge outlays and debts for student loans. Overall, we estimate, as shown later in this article that the impact of the delay in starting work costs the U.S. economy close to $1 trillion dollars per year in output in 2010. However, there are other detrimental effects such as the lack of skilled workers, particularly for manufacturing, etc. and other professionals as well as lower productivity in many sectors of the economy, such as manufacturing, agriculture, and

even some services which more than low cost of labor cause outsourcing. For example, in most other countries, skilled workers such as nurses, secretaries, construction workers, plumbers, electricians, software designers, and more start a 1-2 year professional course right after high school and not after college. As a result, they quality for a professional license at age 19-20, while in the U.S. most do this training only after 4 years of liberal arts college, and then start work at age 22-23. Not only is this a gross waste of time and money, but it also affects people's job or work attitude which in turn affects their productivity.

2.8.1 THE NEW FOR-PROFIT EDUCATION SYSTEMS AND SUB-PRIME CRISIS

These developments are now accelerating with large scale development of "For-Profit colleges or universities" which have very low admission standards, low quality of teaching and programs that are often not recognized. Though they charge as much or more than public colleges, the credentials they award successful graduates are often not recognized and in recent years the bulk (83%) of their graduates were unable to find jobs in the area of their education. Such students were a result unable to repay their student loans.

Such institutions now enroll millions of students who pay high tuition fees and delay their entry into the job markets by 3 plus years. Summarizing the impacts of these sub-prime educational developments, we find

    a. Development of for-profit colleges has increased the percentage of high school leavers who continue a college education for another 3-4 years from 72.8% in 1995 to over 83.6% at the end of 2010. This also caused a significant drop in trade school and community college attendance which in turn caused a drop in qualified professionals for industrial and manufacturing. (Lack of an adequate number of trained, skilled manufacturing and other workers today is a greater driving force for outsourcing than lower labor costs.)

    b. The percentage of un-repaid or non-collectible student loans has nearly doubled in the last 5 years alone. The cost to the taxpayer of uncollectible government guaranteed student loans is now estimated to exceed $10b/year and growing by about 10% annum.

    c. Social Security loses about 7% of expected contributions based on U.S. demographics, yet must pay full benefits even as contributions were paid over 3-4 fewer years than expected.

d. Driving such a large percentage of unmotivated high school graduates towards an unfocused college education instead of directing them towards a career appropriate to their intellectual and motivational objectives and capabilities deprives them of a career path direction and the USA of people to fill satisfying jobs are capable of performing. The lack of young people interested in industrial and manufacturing jobs is today the principal factor driving outsourcing. It is no longer lower U.S. labor costs but the lack of manufacturing and industrial labor or people interested in making a career in industry and manufacturing.

This is a dangerous trend as there is a limit to the size of or percentage of people working in the service industry. Furthermore service functions can be and are increasingly being automated or at least replaced by electronic or information technology which means that there will be a declining demand for service workers. The total impact of for-profit college education and the drift of the majority of people into liberal arts and other non-professional or skill development educational programs will be that we all not only incur increasing government deficits due to un-repaid student loans, declining contributions to Social Security and other support programs, demand for government supported health care and similar programs.

The increasing loss of young workers and particularly workers for industry, agriculture, and other productive output activities are making America increasingly dependent on foreign imports to satisfy American consumption. This is unsustainable in the long run and can only result in the loss of real estate and values transferred to pay increasing foreign debts until all assets are owned by foreign interests.

We are rapidly moving towards this situation and the new sub-prime education environment will or is accelerating the process. For-profit "higher" education is accelerating the process and now involves millions of students who could and should probably be part of the workforce and not victims of a serious fraud which robs them of their time, money, and in a way their future. Much of this trend is driven by the lack of intelligently fostered student motivation. And the cause is not lack of teachers as the student-teacher ratio in U.S. schools has dropped from 27 to 1 in 1955 to 15 to 1 today.

Similarly, teachers are by and large better trained, have better facilities, and resources. What are lacking are effective guidance, good peer examples, and most importantly parental concern and involvement as well as meaningful good role models and incentives. There is too much emphasis on material goals and too little on intellectual, cultural, and spiritual achievements. Competition and achievements are mostly driven by hollow short-term glory and not meaningful achievements which provide longer term improvements and rewards.

There is an urgent need to orient educational programs more towards the development of student intellect, curiosity, and knowledge and leave out sectarian, political correctness, and narrow, unrealistic achievement goals. This may require a different school environment and curricula which emphasize more arts, music, intellectual discussion, and meaningful motivation. Goals must become less materialistic and emphasize as well as reward s must be given to intellectual and not largely to physical or materialistic achievements. To generate student's motivation and interest in a career or profession, they must be involved in activities that generate a real interest in and understanding of different work or professional career opportunities.

Findings of GAO Investigation of For Profit Universities and Colleges

1. Cheating or deception in filling out financial aid applications and encouraging students to lie.
2. Overpriced programs and certification.
3. Encourage applicants to cheat on loan applications.
4. Issue worthless certificates and other credentials.
5. Dismal success in placing or assisting graduates in job searches.
6. Non-transferable credits or degrees.
7. Up to 90% of for profit college revenues is from federally guaranteed student loans (Federal Student Aid) excluding the GI bill and other programs which probably bring the percentage to closer to 100%. In other words, the taxpayer pays.

2.8.2 Rebuilding America's Education

America used to have one of the most effective and admired education systems. Its primary and secondary schools were excellent and many of its universities were and some still are the best in the world. In fact, America developed the concept of research universities and much of the technologies which made the 20th century such a boom for mankind were born and developed in these research universities. Most of the technologies which dominate the world today and made much of mankind so much more effective and content originated and still originates today in the research universities.

However, the educational environment in America has changed in the past few decades. The quality of our primary and secondary education has declined and in many areas, particularly math and science, the lifeblood of technical and modern life and development, our students are falling precipitously behind those in many even poor developing countries.

As noted, America's educational system is highly complex and the quality of education varies widely. Even though America spends more on education in both real and relative terms than any other country in the world or in history, the quality of education has been declining at all levels in recent years. This notwithstanding radical changes at all levels of the education system. Education in America is complex and involves all levels of government, private industry, and social as well as religious organizations and interests.

Primary and secondary education, for example, are usually managed and financed at the very local level such as a village or town district. As a result, the quality of education as well as facilities for education is dependent on the economic condition of the locality. In Boston, for example, the difference in school funding per student may vary as a factor of 3 to 4, with poorer districts receiving or managing with a fraction of the funding richer neighborhoods obtain. This notwithstanding the fact that home, parental and neighborhood support for pupils or students is usually better in richer neighborhoods.

The current (2010) financial crisis was mainly caused by encouraging people to accept loans and mortgages they could not afford. We now face a similar problem in education where we encourage an increasing number of young people to spend 4 years of their life after high school in college and assume a student loan debt for a college education they cannot absorb, afford or effectively use or repay.

As a result, a large number, if not a majority of these students are not able to obtain an appropriate job or benefit otherwise from the expenditure of 10% of their working life and a huge amount of debt they could not and cannot afford or service. In fact, many of them did not and do not have the intellectual or emotional aptitude to benefit from

2.9 AMERICA'S AGRICULTURE

American agricultural policy is not only outdated but also counter-incentive in encouraging the demise of the American farmer and growth of industrialized farming which, while rewarding a minute group, is bad for the U.S. economy, its environment, and its international reputation. The basic farm policies incorporated in the $286b farm bill include loans, price supports, subsidized insurance, and various other aids, such as money for not farming, disaster aid, and more.[7]

Farm Aid was introduced by President Roosevelt about 75 years ago as a temporary measure to help farmers during the Depression and what was called the Dust Bowl period, but conditions today are vastly different. Today the farm bill is one great give away with the top 10% of subsidized farmers collecting 75% of all subsidies. Little if any of this aid goes to small farmers. Considering U.S. agriculture in general only 39% of farms receive subsidies with the top 10% of those averaging $34,190, while the bottom 80% average $704 per year (in 2004).

In general, large commodity groups have a strong hold on policy. Farming today does not attract the young. Less than 6% of American farmers are 35 years or younger and 20% are over 65, this largely because it is very hard today to get started in farming. There are too many vested interests. Now only 1 in 150 is a farmer and of those less than one-third are full-time farmers. We now also have counter-cyclical support to help farmers in bad years. Our farm subsidies artificially reduce world commodity prices such as cotton and more, affecting growers in developing countries. The 2007 farm bill cost every American $189. Much of this money went to macro farmers such as Riceland Foods Inc., which received over $541 million since 1995.

After decades of yield or productivity gains particularly in food grain production, we now face not only large scale diversion of food grain to ethanol production, but also a severe decline in the rate of growth of yields.[8] Average annual productivity growth of food grains

---

[7] Granwald, Michael, "Down on the Farm", U.S. Agricultural Policy is bad for the country's economy, environment, and global image and rural towns, *Time*, November 12, 2007.

[8] Bras, Javier, "The End of Abundance: Food panic brings calls for a second green revolution", FT, June 2, 2008.

has now in 2008 slowed to 0.8-2.0%, gains which cannot sustain the output growth demanded by population increase and growing per capita demands from nearly developed countries.

The pace of yield improvements in the development of new types of seeds, bio-technology or genetically modified crops, water supply, pesticides, and fertilizers has not only slowed but in many cases actually been reserves.

Agricultural development aid has actually declined, while demand has risen by nearly 2% per year. All of this has caused the UN Food and Agricultural Organization Price Index to more than double between 2000 and 2008. Similarly, the U.S., once the world's bread chamber, has become increasingly dependent on imported food. Initially just seasonal fruits and vegetables, but more recently meat, poultry, milk products, and fruits are being imported. While this in part is due to the lack of or high cost of agricultural labor, there are other reasons as well such as government policies, ill-fated bio-fuel projects or policies, and much more.

America is still a major grain, poultry, beef, wine, and fruit producer, and in many areas has captured major markets. Most of these are in labor-extensive agricultural activities where large productive equipment can be used. Large-scale industrialized farming has taken over much of the Midwest and southern areas.

U.S. farm product exports have now declined to less than 10% of total exports which in turn have declined significantly as a percentage of the GDP of America. In fact, this traditional mainstay of the U.S. economy has suffered a significant decline due to a combination of misplaced government policy, lack of investment, and a declining agricultural work force.

2.9.1 Agricultural Performance

Soaring 2008 food prices sent the 41 poorest countries into a negative shock resulting in a decline of their GDP by 3-10% and widespread famine, in addition to forced borrowing to not only purchase urgently needed food but also seeds and fertilizer for small farmers.

The U.S. which had been a major low cost producer greatly reduced its grain exports as bio-fuel production increased the value and reduced availability of grain for food and feed. The world's total meat supply in 1961 was 71m tons and in 2007 about 284m tons or four times as large.

The per capita meat consumption therefore increased nearly two and a half fold.

At the same time, the percentage of grain production used for meat growing grew more than five fold. We today grow and kill nearly 10b animals per year or about 15% of the world's total. In other words, the average human consumes nearly 2 animals per year. However, meat production requires a lot of grain which then vanishes from the grain supply for human consumption and drives up grain prices. This trend cannot continue without affecting the overall and particularly America's economy. Agriculture has always been a mainstay of the American economy, but has been losing its prominence and contribution lately.

There are fewer and fewer small owner operated farms in America. In part, the result of intrusion of real estate developments and industrial uses which have driven up the value of real estate including agricultural land. Other reasons are climatic changes, and lack of affordable and reliable water supply. In fact, America is important an increasing percentage of its food demand and the value of its food imports may soon exceed food exports, a complete reversal of its traditional role.

There are important lessons for us in Brazil, another major traditional food (grain, cattle, etc.) producer and exporter who also got into bio-fuels in a big way and actually managed to meet the bulk of its gasoline (automobile) demand from bio-fuels. Yet at the same time Brazil was able to vastly increase the acreage used for grain production.

Brazil has developed effective approaches for efficient production of crops traditionally grown in temperate climates. In fact, Brazil with a largely tropical climate has developed seeds and planting methods which provide comparable, if not better yields. With year-round growing seasons, Brazil can have several harvests per year.

American agriculture is under severe attach now that its scale and technological advantages are being eroded or even improved upon by others. High American land values, costs of water, labor, and fertilizer are reducing or even reversing many of its traditional competitive advantages. As a result, many American farmers or growers are moving abroad. Agriculture, one of the mainstays of the American economy for so long, is in real danger of losing its competitive advantage and, as a result, market share.

2.10 CRIME AND PUNISHMENT IN AMERICA

The American legal system is highly weighed against small and petty criminals, while big criminals often get away with pats on their hands. For example, there are many cases where people were convicted for insider trading and defrauding investors. Several recent cases of insider training, such as the conviction of Martha Stewart who saved herself $45,000 by using insider information to sell some company shares before negative information on that company was made public, was convicted to 5 months in jail and additional time under house arrest and other restrictions. However, recently Angelo Marcelly, CEO of Countrywide, the nation's largest mortgage company responsible for much of the sub-prime mortgage disaster and in fact one of the originators of the sub-prime mortgage sales scheme who pocketed large fortunes from this business got away with a slap on the hand and was able to maintain much of his gains.

Justice in America is largely aimed at capital offenses and petty criminals, with wealthy, influential, evil doers often slipping through the system. In America if you want to steal, make it big, and worthwhile. The system has no pity or compassion for petty criminals.

In many other countries, law enforcement, public security, and judicial authorities are under one jurisdiction, usually the judicial system of a central government. In America, we have not only a multi-tier system from local district to state and then federal level; we have a similar hierarchy in law enforcement with local police, sheriffs, and state police departments and then a range of federal law enforcement agencies. Few Americans know who is responsible for what. The same applies to the various federal investigative agencies like the FBI, CIA, and many more. There was an attempt to secure coordination by the establishment of the Federal Department of Homeland Security but this was not really accomplished because the Justice Department and Department of Defense continue to control important intelligence, investigative, and law enforcement agencies or functions.

2.10.1 AMERICAN JUSTICE

A few years ago famed fashion and interior artist Martha Stewart was convicted of insider trading (saving her about $45,000) and then lying about it. She was sent to jail for 5 months plus some house arrest. Now the former CFO of Countrywide was convicted of insider trading involving billions and was convicted to pay a fine of $67 million, a very small fraction of the money he made or stole with his unlawful activities. These only show the fallacies of our judicial system which proves that if you steal or cheat make it big enough if you want to stay out of jail if caught.

American jails are full of petty criminals and small recreational drug users who are largely incarcerated not because they are a danger to the public, but for their own good or safety. We could save tens of billions of dollars, increase productive output, and help rehabilitation by using other means of punishment and rehab, such as supervised work programs, national service, and social support work. There are many organizations that require help and could use supervised workers to perform meaningful jobs in the public interest such as maintenance of public spaces such as parks, beaches, rest areas, homeless shelters, and more.

We incarcerate more people than other developed nations yet are no more successful in rehabilitation or the curbing of unlawful or criminal activities.

2.10.2 Frivolous Use of the Justice System

America has nearly twice as many lawyers than engineers or doctors and continues to graduate lawyers in these proportions. While in most Western countries, lawyers practice law and provide legal advice, representation, and various legal services in contract, criminal, and related areas where decisions are subject to laws and regulations. In most countries, lawyers expect clients to ask for help, advice or representation, but the initiative is usually with the client unless lawyers are assigned a case or a client by a judge, court of law or government agency.

America is fairly unique in the way lawyers and law firms market themselves and look after clients, deals, and work. In fact, not only do lawyers in the U.S. market themselves but may go aggressively and proactively after new clients. In fact, the term "ambulance chasing" as a method for marketing legal service is fairly uniquely American. Malpractice and similar claims provide huge possibilities for claims and rewards. In parallel, American lawyers engage in large-scale "Class Actions" where they identify and round up large numbers of possible claimants for damages caused by medical actions, drug (users) performance, product deficiencies or some operational or service performance which can be shown to have caused some damage or cost to a group of users.

Lawyers usually charge or obtain a third of any damages recuperated plus expenses which makes this type of activity or practice very lucrative. In fact, a significant proportion of court and law enforcement agency time and costs are spent on these types of "legal" activities. In most other countries, these issues are often resolved by expert arbitration, with the legal establishment only brought in to assist with enforcement actions, if necessary. Similarly, American lawyers are involved in many activities that are either not used necessary or done by others in different countries. These include product and operational safety environmental protection and many more.

The cost of legal services and some may say security and justice in America is very high in economic, political, and other terms. Activities, actions, and operations in any field are performed much more defensively in America in response to the ever present threat of legal claims. It is hard to determine the total economic, financial, social, and cultural costs of the defensiveness which is requires in anything, but these direct and indirect costs are enormous and not just in fiscal but also societal, technological, cultural, and basic human quality of life terms.

While lawyers are usually politically active throughout the world, they are much more deeply involved not just in the political processes, such as elections, but are usually very active in lobbying, policy analysis and design, strategic studies, the design of laws and regulations, and their administration and oversight. While most of these activities or involvement may be legitimate functions and responsibilities for lawyers, their involvement in America goes much further. Most importantly, lawyers in America are much more proactive. There is a serious question if this is in the public interest and contributes to the quality of life and order in a democratic society.

An increasing number of lawsuits generated by law firms to increase business are clogging our court systems and cost taxpayers billions in money without any corresponding benefit to society or the economy. In fact, it is amazing how U.S. law firms invent and market both individual and class suits on issues which have been ignored or were unknown to cause any personal or societal damage. Billions are now spent on frivolous marketing and the law enforcement and court systems are clogged with these types of cases, all to increase lawyer revenues.

There should be a charge to law firms to place cases on a court docket and they should similarly be required to prepay costs of investigation by police and other public investigative agencies, with money returned only if the case is settled by a court ruling which determines the legitimacy of the case. In other words, law firms should be required to put money sufficient to cover public agency (courts, police, etc.) costs in escrow until the case is adjudicated and found to be a legitimate complaint. If not so found, the cost of all public efforts by courts, police, etc. would be charged to that account.

2.10.3 Range of American Lawyer Activities

While most lawyers in America practice law, a significant number work as government officials, administrators, judges, and legal advisors. However, many also work in industry, financial services, law enforcement, lobbying, lawmaking (politicians), and more. In fact, it is estimated that less than half the registered lawyers in America actually practice law.

A law degree is increasingly being considered as an entry pass to a whole array of attractive jobs or careers. Many senior officials in the banking, industry, and various services are people with legal backgrounds who found their law degree with or without legal experience an excellent stepping stone to a career in these different areas.

Lawyers have made big business out of medical and other malpractice, but are seldom charged with legal malpractice. However, there are many cases of bad legal advice, strategy or procedure which often causes cheats or the public horrendous harm in economic, social or other terms such as, for example, loss of freedom when unjustly convicted because of some lawyer's legal failure or malpractice. There is an urgent need to extend malpractice procedures to the legal profession, including lawyers, law enforcers, as well as court systems. The legal profession has for too long been exempted from critical scrutiny and responsibility for their action or inaction.

Our legal system has to be reconstituted into a true justice system, with rewards and penalties fairly and honestly conveyed. As in financial services where we are aghast at the fact of obscene bonuses paid for success in risking other people's money, but no similar negative bonus or penalty in case of failure or loss, we urgently need a system in the judicial system of rewards and penalties where lawyers cannot only cash in but may also risk their own time and money.

As an example, let us look at a typical class action where a law firm spends a few thousand dollars to make a case after identifying a potential victim such as a pharmaceutical company, medical practitioner or manufacturer, then gets lists of thousands of potentially affected users and gets them to spend many hours of work to make or support the case which when won will give the law firm a windfall, while the so-called injured parties get pennies for each hour they spent to make or support the case for the suing law firm.

The same applies to accidents and malpractice suits. However, if the lawyers do not succeed, there is no penalty over and above the small effort and expense spent in identifying and making the case. In other words, just as in the case of the banker or broker, it is a case where the originator or gambler always wins or loses very little, but is never held accountable for the large losses or risks of the actually damaged parties.

2.10.4 REWARDS AND PUNISHMENT

A major and increasing problem in America is that society, our economic as well as justice system, emphasize reward but not punishment. This is not only true in our financial services where people get rewards and bonuses if money was made, but pay no penalty when money was lost due to their actions. The same is true throughout American society. When physical or infrastructure is built, engineers, developers, and investors are rewarded, but when it fails hardly anyone is punished. The New Orleans levees did not just fail, they were not maintained though there were ample resources to maintain and rebuild them.

There are many examples of failed infrastructure, social, and service systems which can be traced directly to human failure, omission or in many cases outright corruption. But even if the damage and loss of human life, perpetrators get at most a pat on the hand and rarely go to prison. This approach to justice is counter-incentive and encourages crime and corruption on an ever increasing scale.

While America used to have and enforce a rational criminal justice system in the past, it has now been so distorted that it provides increasing incentives to all kinds of criminals or crooks and many lawyers make a living not upholding the law but providing cover for offenders. We really need a criminal punishment system instead of our criminal justice system and make it increasingly expensive to commit criminal acts against persons, property, and the public at large.

Our judicial system is too heavily based on protecting and often even rewarding criminals. This too is extreme where now criminals and criminal activities become role models not just for the young but even professionals in finance, engineering, and more. Even our political systems and organizations have been significantly undermined with shady activities and operations.

Lobbying, which used to be done primarily by citizens and their organizations, is now done primarily by professional, well financed lobbyists. In fact, few if any citizens can gain access to politicians, government officials or departments and other law or decision makers without hiring or using a lobbyist or other facilitator any more. We essentially have democracy run amok. I have tried for weeks to gain electronic, verbal or written access to lawmakers or government officials only to find full mailboxes, schedules, and returned mail. Officially Washington representatives are supposed to be there for us the citizen, but in reality they act and are mainly available to special interests. This is not democracy and certainly not what our founding fathers planned or hoped for.

This also encourages increasing unethical and sometimes criminal behavior by lawmakers and public officials. Is it any wonder that people in general are completely disenchanted by the two ruling parties who do not seem to understand or represent the people at large? We need a people's party, not a tea, green, democratic or republican party. We need a justice system not for justice for the criminals, but justice for the people — justice for the average American in a physical, social, economic, and opportunity sense. This country has never been as divided as it is now — socially, economically, politically, and culturally. Our prisons are full of petty criminals and small drug offenders, while the real murderers, thieves, and cheats get rewarded or end up with a slap on the hand. Robin Hood's old mantra that it is more dangerous to steal an apple than to kill a neighbor holds true as never before.

Our justice and regulatory system allowed Madoff and Enron to ruin thousands of people for decades and corrupt financial managers who gamble with other people's money pay themselves and are being rewarded with millions even when they lose much of their investor's money, but they are never penalized, even when they lose investor's money. We better recognize that America allows one of the most corrupted systems in the world, which in the end is much more harmful to Americans and our economy than the petty corruption we always decry in other countries. Yet neither our legal system nor government is willing or able to deal with it or even denounce it. In fact, it appears that much of our legislature and government if not in cahoots with those people and organizations at least let it happen so as not to rock the boat or shut off the tap.

2.10.5 Lobbying in America

Lobbying is a typical part of the political and legislative system in America. There are over 11,000 lobbyists full time in Washington who spend close to $4 billion dollars largely on influencing; they would say informing, lawmakers about pending decisions. In other words, we have about 20 lobbyists per lawmaker. This by the way excludes the Washington law firms and representatives of various companies and organizations, including a large number of foreign interests not directly part of foreign delegations. Similarly, there are numerous civil, business, and professional as well as social organizations and associations in Washington whose prime function is to influence lawmakers.

Lobbying and other forms of influence peddling which usually goes far beyond distribution and expansion of information and is often designed to influence lawmaking directly as well as provide direct economic benefits to the interested parties really undermines basic principles of democracy and often hurts the public, as public and sponsor interests rarely coincide.

Many lobbyists really work in opposition to the public interest and the public at large. In addition, American politicians are affected, if not influenced, by direct contributions to and help in their election or re-election campaigns. Most Western democratic countries have strict rules applied to lobbying with restrictions not only on amounts and purpose of direct financial support but also the use of actual contributions. The most dangerous recent development is the Supreme Court's ruling that corporations like individuals can and should not be restricted in their contributions to political parties, including foreign companies.

3.0 American Economy

The American economy has been in decline for several years now. While the sub-prime mess and the housing crisis are usually blamed for it, the problems are much deeper and much more persistent. The economy lost many of its traditional mainstays such as a vibrant manufacturing industry, low cost competitive agriculture, and more. Sectors such as textiles, shipbuilding, and even pharmaceuticals were increasingly outsourced and then moved abroad. Emerging economies became not only increasingly outsourced but also competed increasingly in the raw materials and parts or components markets. Domestic policies such as the use of food grains for fuel production, farming subsidies which often paid farmers not to produce increasingly undermined the U.S. agricultural sector. Once the envy of the world and the global bream chamber America now imports increasing volumes of agricultural products and other food items.

In the 90s many emerging economies faced major problems, with huge national financial crises hitting countries in Central and South America as well as Asia. One after another of these countries' economies collapsed and as predicted by Professor Nouriel Roabini, America would follow[9] not only because of the exuberance in its housing and financial markets but also because of the lack of rigorous enforcement of regulations and laws. In fact, the oversight of most federal agencies during the last ten years was fragmented with most or too many politicians, government officials, and industry leaders opting to let the market regulate itself.

As Roabini rightly mentioned, America does not only have a sub-prime housing but a sub-prime financial systems crisis. America for years experienced current account deficits which by 2004 exceeded $600. Its foreign trade deficits resulted in the accumulation of foreign debts in the trillions of dollars. America was not only the world's largest economy, but the world's largest debtor. More and more American assets were acquired by foreign investors and more and more interest payments on foreign-held

---

9 Mhim, Stephen, "Dr. Doom", about Professor Nouriel Roabini, The New York Times Magazine, August 17, 2008.

government and other debt instruments were paid to foreign interests, accelerating the rate of growth of American foreign debts.

Traditional economics use forecasts based largely on past trends and often ignore potential, even likely developments, which may lead to radically different results. As many contend, economists are actually a very optimistic bunch, seldom predicting bad developments even when these appear likely. For example, the housing crisis, once it hit, was estimated to cost the financial industry and economy tens of billions of dollars, a sum later revised by Congress to $300 billion, the sum noted by housing legislation-sponsored by Senator Dodd and Representative Frank. Since then, government had to take over the two major private yet government sponsored mortgage institutions (Freddie Mac and Fannie Mae[10]) which may expose taxpayers to even larger sums. In fact, government may have to take over or bail out or take over not only mortgage lenders but many regional as well as national banks as well as the foreclosed assets on their books at a cost of trillions of dollars.

There is no doubt that the American economy is in a recession now in the fall of 2010 and that the global linkages of the financial industry will cause the recession to spread to Europe and some Asian countries. In parallel, inflationary trends, rapid increases in the cost of fuel and food will drag many developing and underdeveloped country economies into recession as well which may drag on for years.

The American economy has become too dependent on consumer spending, particularly as much of it is for imported goods, including recently increasingly food, electronics, games, and appliances which used to be largely made in America. The spending therefore increases our foreign debt as our exports cover only a fraction of the costs of our imports. The recent weak dollar policy which is supposed to make U.S. exports more competitive is actually working, but it has a very undesirable secondary effect on making American assets cheap to foreigners who as a result are buying up huge amounts of valuable U.S. assets from real estate to manufacturing, farming, and service assets. Some of the most valuable American assets are now foreign owned and much of the profits as well as capital gains they generate will probably be exported to the owner's countries. These are therefore both short and long term effects of the current crisis which may affect the American economy as well as living standards for some time.

---

10 Freddie Mac and Fannie Mae are government sponsored enterprises (GSEs) owned by private investors.

There is something seriously wrong with the reward system in the financial service industry which considers only obscene rewards but ignores risks. The rewards or bonuses are taken for granted while the risks are something to be transferred to the unsuspecting public, taxpayers are others. It does not matter if profits are just paper profits and not real in the long run, the game goes on and the bonuses are claimed, even if the shareholders and sometimes even the depositors lose out.

In fact, many aspects of the American financial system are misleading or outright dishonest. Brokers who offer low "commissions" for example usually fail to mention the fees or kickbacks they get from traders and market makers which often add significantly more to the costs of transactions than fixed commissions would. While these practices are common in the securities trade, they are also practiced in real estate and all kinds of other transactions. In fact, the commission or kickback games have become the lifeblood of much of the American financial and brokerage systems. These in addition to the many so-called derivatives, securitization, and other schemes, many of which are designed not to improve the markets but to permit unearned and often misleading gains for the developers and underwriters of such schemes are a major reason for the serious recent failures of the financial markets. While most originated in the U.S., foreign banks and institutions were drawn in as well by the prospects of huge profits. Greed overwhelmed reason and judgment and much of the world's financial institutions were as a result sucked into the downstream once the house of cards collapsed with the bursting of the American as well as other housing markets.

Recovery of the near global recession now depends on a reliable confirmation of a bottom of the U.S. real estate market, something which may take some time and will probably not happen before the second half of 2011. The recovery of housing and other largely American asset values may actually drag on further as global confidence in the health of the American economy continues to wane and as the U.S. increases its reliance for loans and investments. In fact, it may require large new inflows to help cover the Fannie Mae, Freddie Mac, Bear Stearns, AIG, and other bailouts which will really stretch government capabilities as the government now holds the bulk of U.S. mortgages.

Together with the continued drain on government funds by the Iraq and Afghanistan wars, and a budget deficit, America faces continuing needs for foreign borrowing with an associated transfer of American assets. While the government rescues of failed financial institutions may regain some public and foreign confidence in the American economy, there are long term implications well beyond the evident transfer of assets abroad. These are both economic and political and in the long run will greatly reduce American influence, power, and the ability to lead the world. The takeover of the U.S. mortgage giants essentially puts the government in control of nearly three quarters of the domestic mortgage market and as a consequence a large chunk of real assets of the economy. The government has added $5.4 trillion to its gross liabilities which is equal to the existing publicly held debt and 40% of GDP. Major Western countries and particularly the U.S. now maintain very small foreign exchange reserves as shown in Table 3.

Table 3: Selected Foreign Exchange Reserves and Sovereign Wealth Funds (December 31, 2007) (Source: Morgan Stanley and IMF)

Country	Foreign Exchange (official)	Sovereign Wealth Fund
U.S.	47	40
Canada	30	45
Australia	26	49
New Zealand	15	10
China	1100	200
Russia	350	141
UAE	27.5	750
Kuwait	20	180
Saudi Arabia	23.2	200
Norway	330	46
Japan	900	—

The major Western countries and particularly America are woefully short of reasonable foreign exchange reserves and sovereign wealth funds which are a sign of economic prowess and an ability to influence markets.

America used to be the world's premier exporter but has been overtaken by both Germany and China in recent years, with Japan not far behind[11]. America's foreign trade imbalance of more than $600b/year in recent times has shrunk somewhat as a result of the economic recession and the decline in the value of the dollar, but this may not persist with a new strengthening of the dollar. At the same time, improved vehicle fuel efficiency and use of alternative fuels and energy may level off or even reduce American petroleum imports which should allow a decline in the foreign trade imbalance.

The economic crisis of 2008 has brought many companies in America to their knees. First, the financial services and similar self-serving institutions including banks, private equity, insurance, and others clamor for federal government assistance and bail out claiming that the American and probably world economy would suffer or collapse unless the taxpayers stepped in and saved them from collapse resulting largely from excessive risk taking, bad management, and sometimes outright corruption.

Hardly had the government stepped into this breach with hundreds of billions of dollars when two of the big three U.S. automakers ran to Washington demanding $25b of bail out money to top up the $25b already authorized to help them modernize their plants. The claim was that if they were not to survive the economic crisis, millions of jobs would be lost. These included, in addition to the 250,000 direct employees (down from over half a million just a few years ago), 750,000 employees of dealers, and 1-2 million working for suppliers, and others.

The assumption was apparently that if the big three were to go under Americans would no longer make or buy automobiles, while recent history shows that in fact foreign auto makers are doing quite well manufacturing cars in America, usually using U.S. workers under union contracts. There is an urgent need in America for more corporate oversight and involvement of shareholders in major strategic decisions as well as in setting executive compensation, including bonus allocations.

These decisions are too important to be left to the sole discretion of executives and boards which are often appointed or selected by management. The reasons are that management and boards are often found to be self-serving and opportunistic instead of having the corporations and its owners (shareholders) and workers primary interests in mind.

---

11   Zamaria, Fareed, "The Post American World", Norton, 2008, New York.

The American economy is increasingly driven by consumption; yet as an increasing percentage of goods, food, energy, and now even services, Americans buy are foreign imports, this is a false strategy as it only increases America's debt to foreign countries. Consumption has become the driving force of the American economy and is growing at a dangerous pace, largely driven by government policies and incentives. In fact, not long ago, the government decided to give each citizen $250 in cash to spend under the erroneous assumption that this would help restart growth of the faltering U.S. economy. I suggested to Washington to save the postage and send the money directly to China by wire, as the impact would be the same.

America has lost much of its manufacturing and even agricultural capacity. Even an increasing percentage of services are now imported. This is unsustainable and will not only continue to increase foreign debt which stands already at an unsustainable level, but also an increasing transfer of real assets abroad which will increase America's dependence. While America still leads in military power and technology development, others are catching up and even these advantages may soon vanish.

3.0.1 American Economic Developments

America's economy has undergone radical changes in the last 20 years, with little of the old economy left. We now have 3-4 times as many security guards than machinists and many more casino card dealers than lathe operators. In fact, people in service jobs outnumber manufacturing workers 8 to 1 and farm workers 60 to 1. In other words, less than 16% of working Americans do productive jobs, the rest are occupied in services, government, arts, security, military, fashion, and so on. This puts the country at a distinct disadvantage as there are not enough people to produce things we consume and need nor those capable of building and maintaining the physical infrastructure which provides the lifeblood of America's economy. While services are important and needed in a modern society, America has gone overboard in its reliance on services to fuel its economy. It is too large to concentrate so much on such narrow sectors of the economy and become dependent on others for most manufacturing, construction, maintenance, and other activities.

America's GDP growth has been on a long run decline since 1980, a trend that will continue for the foreseeable future. Its economy will also continue to be very cautious after the huge losses sustained by lenders as a result of sub-prime mortgage, securitization, and other problems faced by the finance industry. Though these problems originated in America, they now encompass much of the world and will take a long time to be resolved. The results of these early 21st century problems will have more lasting effects and may affect America's controlling role in the global economy.

In parallel, Americans in general now have not only a sense of economic but also political insecurity. They can feel an unaccustomed lack of control over their economic and social conditions and an increasing concern with economic injustice. Most income gains in recent years were obtained by the top earners in the society. In fact, 75% of all income addition went to the 1% top earners in America, with many particularly among the poor with no gains at all. In fact, the situation is even more dramatic with only 0.01% of all Americans controlling much of the total income. There is an increasing feeling of inequality with average people struggling to just keep up and a miniscule portion of the population rewarding themselves with obscene amounts.[12]

These obscene incomes are not earned by the most productive people or those contributing greatly to the economy but by and large by those gambling with or within our financial system. It is no longer the captains of industry who earn a lot but the people who have distorted and undermined our financial system. Few could justify their earnings by pointing to their contributions to the American economy. At the same time, the government continues with deficit spending with a deficit exceeding $500b looming for the 2008 financial year. This is a deficit of 3.5% of GDP.

There is also little chance for an early reversal of government deficits even if the ill-advised war in Iraq will come to an end in one or two years (by 2011). The high cost of energy imports, American housing crisis demands for imports in general, and lack of extensive output for export in addition to difficult to reverse and costly tax breaks will make it difficult for a speedy economic recovery to be achieved. As noted elsewhere in this book, we similarly suffer under increased health care, retirement, education, and law enforcement costs which will continue to haunt our economy for a long time.

---

12 Fox, Justin, "How the Next President Should Fix the Economy:, *Time*, May 26, 2008.

Ernst G. Frankel

3.0.1.1 America's Do-it-yourself Economy

We are all aware that more and more jobs are being outsourced to low or lower labor cost countries, but there is another development which may have even more lasting effects on the American society and economy and that is the increasing self-serve culture. Not only do we gas up ourselves, swipe our credit card through a reader, check our own sugar, blood pressure or even HIV, check in at airports and rail/bus stations, and deposit or withdraw funds at banks without a teller, we are now confronted by automated telephone or Internet answering services which waste huge amounts of our time to book something or get some information just to save the paid server a few cents for live service.

The situation has become so bad that most of us now spend many times as much to transact routine services only to save the paid supplier a pittance in expenses. This situation is permeating all sectors of the U.S. economy. In class action courts and lawyers expect the supposed damaged investors to customers to spend hours or days extracting and submitting information so that they can sue the supposed contravener to be prosecuted and they are rewarded with hundreds of millions in largely unearned fees while the damaged investors are lucky if they get the equivalent of one or two cents for each hour they spent in building up the case.

America's role as the world's economic locomotive has not only been exaggerated but has also declined to a minor level. Its share of world imports dropped from 19% to 14% just in the last few years. At the same time, most emerging country economies have grown not just in their roles in international trade but also in robustness. The American housing slump not only affected America's economic growth but together with the sharp increase in the cost of oil has greatly reduced the power of the American consumer who traditionally provided the underlying power of the American economy. Homes have always provided the major credit guarantees for the American consumer, but the decline in their value and increased cost for essentials like energy he no longer can afford to use his home assets to underwrite his traditional consumption.

The American economy needs a serious stimulus or new incentives; yet neither government nor economic/financial leaders seem to have a clear idea or rational plan on how to proceed to not just turn the economy around but give it a new direction in a rapidly changing world. They must recognize that the world did not only change geographically and demographically, but also technically and economically. The economic center of the world is rapidly moving from the West or the Atlantic basin with the U.S. and EU leading in economic capacity and leadership to the Pacific basin and Asia, with China, Japan, and South Asia increasingly advancing their economies. Even in the Atlantic basin there are major changes with Brazil increasing its economic prowess.

Between the two World Wars and right after World War II, America grew from a large developing, former colonial country into a global economic, political, cultural, and social powerhouse. It attracted top talents from all over the world and with the support of huge natural resources was able to become the world's economic locomotive, strategic power, and political beacon, starting with rapid industrialization which transformed the country from a largely agricultural, mining, and resource exploitation economy into a, or the major, industrial power. Starting with automobile production, American industry grew into the global center for heavy equipment, manufacturing, and mining as well as cargo handling machinery and electrical equipment to medical and diagnostic equipment, America became not only the leader but the principal source; this not only for the equipment but also for the technology, operational approach, and systems.

America became truly the economic, technological, and even social and cultural leader of the world. In parallel, it became the world's premier trader responsible for nearly a quarter of world trade (see Figure 1).

As the world's largest trader, U.S. trade was about $2.5 trillion in 2008 and accounted for approximately 22% of the American gross product or economy and about 20% of world trade. Its participation in the global trade has since leveled off and with an increasing trade imbalance and declining dollar it is experiencing now growing difficulties to maintain its position in world trade.

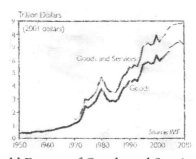

Figure 1: World Export of Goods and Services (1950-2010)

3.0.1.2 Government Intervention in the Free Market

Free markets can only work in honest law abiding, educated societies. Free means no government interference in the commercial or business transactions. This does not mean that the government should only be involved in case of fraudulent, misleading or outright corrupt activities. Freedom in markets should relate to the lack of government control of prices, costs, terms of trade or transactions. Government may and in most cases should be an arbitrator and sometimes enforcer in cases of fraudulent or dishonest practices which undermine truly free and open and honest trade and commerce.

Governments should set the basic rules or conditions on a local, national, and international scale and set the conditions under which trade can be performed. They may also intervene if there is evidence of fraud or other dishonest behaviors designed to give unfair and/or illegal advantage to a party or parties in the trade. The WTO (World Trade Organization) designs and imposes the basic rules and conditions of fair yet free trade which implies free markets in which all parties design and impose rules and conditions of trade. However, when conditions arise where one or more parties (or nations) claims, uses or imposes unfair advantages, then government and/or organizations such as WTO should and will step in to reassert free markets and trade.

3.0.2 Managing America

For a long time, America was known worldwide as the originator and developer of modern management. In fact, management as a science, with well-defined principles and procedures, was an American development. The world's first programs in management and the intellectual and scientific bases for it were developed in America. However, today America which led the way in making management efficient and effective lags much of the world in management. Not only is government at most levels and many institutions grossly mismanaged, but America has largely failed to live up to its own principles and teachings in management.

Though traditional line type management was discredited for a long time, most American organizations, companies, and institutions continue to use line-type management. This is not only inefficient but it also discourages initiative and often causes unjust or absurd reward structures. As Secretary of Defense Gates recently commented, the U.S. military is largely inefficient as it adheres to strict hierarchical organization and management structures, where duties or tasks are often performed by over-qualified people.

In other words, generals do jobs that could and should be done by colonels or majors and so forth. The problem is that this causes not only larger than necessary organizations, but also delays effective or timely decision making. We have similar experience in American industry, services, and more. As a result, an increasing number of U.S. enterprises in manufacturing, services, and even government are now run or operated by foreign enterprises.

3.0.3 Labor, Employment, and Productivity

Israel is a curious labor and work environment. It has some of the world's most and least productive workers, some of the most intelligent and committed work force in parallel with some of the most archaically entrenched backward labor forces. On one hand most private employers have a committed, intelligent workforce. However, in parallel, some public sectors such as ports have some of the world's most backward workforce entrenched in archaic work rules with little incentive to improve productivity or quality of output. Even though the labor unions of Israel, once a powerful political and economic force, are now a micro shadow of their past, they are still able to use threats and other measures such as blockading as a means to not only gain economic advantages, but also prevent any introduction of changes in labor, technology, and work rules. At the same time, the same labor takes full advantage of economic progress and social benefits which their employers can neither afford nor allow without losing many of their users or customers.

In other words, Israel has two labor markets, diametrically opposed. A highly motivated and productive high tech work force which not only achieves a higher productivity than similar workers in other countries and a traditional, old-style work force still imbedded in century old work rules and labor intransigence. The latter primarily abounds in some public sectors, such as ports, electric power, and more; yet unfortunately did not manage to infiltrate other public sectors such as law enforcement and health care.

Unfortunately workers in sectors such as ports, etc. are able to not only seriously impact the economy but also affect labor relations, this notwithstanding the fact that the traditional labor unit, the Histadrat, is now a mere shadow of its storied past. Because of its monopoly position and long-term political prowess, it continues to exert a disproportional role in the economy. Port worker intransient impacts on Israel's trading competitiveness and efficiency of investment. Ports impose limited working hours which affect ship turnaround times and cargo handling rates.

This in turn reduces the amount of cargo including containers that can be handled by each berth or set of gantries per unit time. Restricted working hours make the situation worse and as a result not only are shipping costs higher than necessary but service frequency and delivery times are reduced. Furthermore, the lack of acceptable productivity and throughput generates demands for additional infrastructure investments in piers, gantries, and reclaimed port land for storage, much of which often remains idle for years after investments of hundreds of millions of dollars. The combination of low port productivity, over-investment, and less than efficient ship services has a huge impact on Israel's economy, particularly volume trades, such as citrus exports.

Some studies indicate that it would be economically efficient to simply fire and put on live pension all port workers, under the condition that they do not approach the port or directly and/or indirectly interfere in port operations. The labor situation in Israel's ports is a historic legacy of the formerly ruling labor party which for decades and since Israel's founding in 1948 led Israel's government and political system. The situation is very different now with little of labor unionized which is largely the result of a radical change in Israel's economy which is today much more sophisticated and high technology in all sectors.

3.0.4 AMERICAN TAX COLLECTION SHORTFALLS AND GOVERNMENT WASTE

With all modern electronic information technology, the American tax collectors still miss major evaders. It is estimated that in 2007 there was a tax shortfall (uncollected taxes) of $290b. In addition $2.5n under-taxed and $60b of unwarranted tax breaks bring the shortfall to $352.5b.

Considering wasteful health care expenditures such as fraud and over-payment $60b, unnecessary Medicare administrative costs of $10b, and a 15% cost reduction in Medicare and Medicaid costs as well as closing the 12% loop hole an additional $115b could be saved. In military spending at least $100b were wasted in fraud, unnecessary weapons, etc. Then there are $20b of wasteful farm subsidies, $20b of wasteful capital spending, and $2b in disability and food stamp over-payments, $20b in pork barrel spending, and $50b in corporate welfare, $20b for obsolete or redundant programs for a total of $789.5b. Finally, there is the interest on our historically high national debt of $194b for a total of $983.5b or about 8.4% of our Gross Domestic Product.

American public debt reached over $10 trillion in early 2010, of which over $2 trillion were owed to China. In addition, the U.S. faces the fact that some of its social support programs such as Social Security, Medicare, and others have huge unfunded obligations which in 2010 terms amount to over $50 trillion. As noted by Fareed Zakaria[13], there is no way this country can meet these obligations under existing revenue and expenditure conditions. He suggests rightfully that we must develop and enforce new public revenue streams and curb consumption to more reasonable levels. Most European and some other countries use VAT (Value Added Tax or a sales tax of 12-18%). This not only provides a very significant revenue stream, but also helps to curb rocketing consumption, particularly of unnecessary and luxury goods. It also encourages greater concentration on exportable goods and services. In fact, some countries are also imposing VAT on consumer services such as transport and entertainment.

We already impose sales and meal taxes in many states and such an approach is much more acceptable, fair, and implementable than raising the general tax levels, particularly on low and middle income earners. In addition, many other countries offer incentives for saving to the public, while we offer incentives for consumption which is the worst thing a debt-ridden country like ours can do. Like a family or individual, a nation has to live within its means, with our exports at a historic low as a function of the size of our economy, imports, and government revenues, we will have to bite the bullet and like individuals start to live within our means and spend or consume only what we can afford and less than the value of our output or production. Otherwise our national debts will continue to grow and if we are unable to service and ultimately repay the debt, our lenders may rightfully demand transfer of real assets like buildings, land, etc. In the recent Greek debt crisis, some rightfully suggested that Greece sell or transfer ownership of some of its Aegean islands to foreign creditors, private or sovereign.

---

13 Zakaria, Fareed, "Difussing the Debt Bomd", *Newsweek*, March 8, 2010.

3.0.5 Honesty in Marketing and Advertising

America has led the world in commercial marketing and advertising for many years and officially there are laws of truth in advertising that should apply. However, many ads as well as marketing approaches are not just misleading, but in many cases fraudulent.

1. Inflated first item pricing and free second item to make people think they get extras for free.
2. Advertising of prescription drugs with dangerous warning signs asking people to talk to their doctors into prescribing it.
3. Overpriced shipping and handling tricks not specified (S&H charges often exceed cost of item).
4. False or exaggerated claims in advertising.

Cozy relationships between regulators and industries or companies they are supposed to regulate and keep honest and law abiding. Lack of adequate enforcement, more than lack of regulation is the real culprit.

Some advertisements are outright misleading or even outrageous such as a drug ad which is said to have possible side effects such as suicide, fatal heart attacks, and more, and buyers are asked to call their doctor right away if any of these things happen. So far I have not met dead people able to use a telephone, but on a more serious note the simple recommendation to suggest to one's doctor what medication to use is preposterous and would not be used or even allowed in other countries.

Marketing in America has become a science, with advertisers using fine print and now fine (super fast) talk to mislead people or at least meet legal requirements of "full" disclosure, never mind that listeners could not possibly understand, absorb or remember (or write down) the information given. Advertisements are also increasingly full of half truths, outrageous or unsubstantiated claims.

The same applies to ads or announcements for services where listeners are bombarded with evidently wrong claims all based on the premise or assumption that people all want bargains and feel special or unique. Overpricing one item and then offering a second item or service for free is such a trick. There are also cases of legitimate insurance company claims which assumed that ordinary people are dumb. For example, one offered coverage of treatments for a year with a cap of $1,000, yet required a monthly premium of $100. Obviously the sum of the cost of the premiums exceeded the maximum reimbursement for medical services allowed under the contract and subscribers would be better off just putting the monthly premium into a savings account.

There are no effective laws for marketing and as noted "truth in advertising" laws do not go far enough nor can they be used effectively by individuals. They require class action and as noted such an approach may reward some organizing lawyer but seldom compensates injured consumers or patients.

Marketing consumes a huge percentage of total costs of various products. In some cases, marketing costs may be as large as total research, design, production, raw material, packaging, distribution, and retailing. In other words, advertising/marketing may cost as much as the product or service being sold. It therefore often results in double the real cost and is a major reason why so many U.S. products are so much cheaper outside the U.S.

3.0.6 Prevention versus Correction

Americans are wary of admitting any deficiency. They are loath to admit any shortcomings be it in health, competence, knowledge, and more. For example, African Americans who are known to suffer many heredity medical issues have the fewest physical examinations of any sector of the American population. The same applies to other check ups such as financial, professional, and more. While in many other advanced countries, updating health, financial, professional, and even social records is a routine. Americans in general are loath to undergo check ups. As a result, most Americans are surprised when things happen such as a sudden medical problem, financial or economic setback, loss of job or even marital conflict. We as a nation like to just assume that everything is all right and that nothing needs to be done, least of all a check up.

In part, this is probably driven by our confidence combined with a daily avalanche of news and sayings that not only is everything and everyone all right but that we are the greatest, healthiest, wealthiest, and best in everything. So no check up or remedial action are required. We know we are fine and the best so why check up and possibly kill the dream. We feel better just believing what we are told in a flood of newscasts and pronouncements. But this issue goes further and has greater ramifications.

In today's world, with rapidly changing technology and lifestyle, there is an urgent need to continually update our knowledge and skills.

Unlike most other nations, we perform less retraining, knowledge updating, check ups, and modernization than most advanced nations. We continue to claim that our work force is the most productive even when basic statistics say otherwise; that our technology is the best even when we know that others have overtaken us; claim having the best infrastructure though we did not rebuild or modernize it in over 50 years. We lack modern railways, highways, electric grids, air traffic control systems, and now even modern hospitals, schools, and social service institutions.

We expect people to learn a skill once so that it will last them a lifetime. Few American employers have regular retraining and skill updating programs, while most foreign employers in China, Japan, Germany, etc. do. They send their workers and staff regularly for retraining, skill enhancement, and education to make sure they not only know about the latest technology and methods, but also how it applies to and improves their own work or function.

We must learn to be more honest in judging ourselves from our health, education, social skills, and work performance. The macho American who is best at everything and knows and does everything better is a thing of the past.

3.1 American Capitalism

Americans are proud to designate New York as the World Center of Capitalism and the New York Stock Exchange as its cradle. While Americans such as the Vanderbilts, Rockefellers, Mellons, and others were truly barons of capitalism and developed novel approaches to make capital an effective development tool, many of the so-called end of the 20th century successors of American capitalism have largely distorted the concepts of the use of capital as a principal tool for social and economic development. Instead, capital is now considered by many in the financial industry simply as a tool for personal enrichment without a parallel contribution to development.

American capitalism, as represented by its financial service industry is, to a large extent, is basically a narrow, self-serving industry with singular goals of enriching its practitioners. They invented private equity, venture capital, sub-prime mortgage instruments, securitization, and a whole array of new approaches and derivatives towards concentration of gains by the few, with the risk remaining with the many who were lured into the usually false promises of the organizers who generally risked little if anything but gained the lion share of profits or benefits of the scheme, if any. The risks were always with the unsuspecting investors or public at large. This new concept of American capitalism is not just a distortion of the basic principles of capitalism, but in many cases borders on criminal intent or action.

As a result, capitalism which promises efficient use of capital for social and economic development has become a tool for the few to enrich themselves on account of the many. It is a true distortion of the promise of the American way of life and if allowed to continue will undermine the promise of this great nation. In fact, it is rather disturbing how the public is being brain-washed about the great benefits of American Free Market Capitalism, which I admit it is a truly effective and beneficial economic system but only if practiced in its true basic form envisioned by our founding fathers and as controlled by our Constitution.

Free Market Capitalism is fine and may provide efficient means to assure justice, progress, and prosperity to a maximum number of people, but only if practiced fairly, honestly, and intelligently. It is not a good or fair system if it allows dishonesty, partiality, unfairness, and corruption. The European type of socialism has been derided by many politicians in the U.S. and the role of government in many areas has been questioned; yet we generally find that many of our economic, social, and environmental problems are the result of lack of oversight or government involvement.

3.1.1 Fair Taxation

Having lived in 27 countries in the last 40 years, I am always amazed at how little we pay in taxes in America, this notwithstanding the claim by Republican lawmakers that taxes on business are too high and thereby affect American competitiveness. Most of these claimants seem to know little about tax regimes abroad or purposely use cover up arguments. Most countries maintain graduated income tax which does not top out at 35 or 38% but continues to go up sometimes to as much as 90% of the last dollar in a high salary of tens of millions.

Another issue is that most other countries have much larger consumption and value added taxes. In fact, the average taxpayer in many countries such as Germany or the UK consumption taxes like VAT (15% +) and gasoline taxes often cost taxpayers more than income taxes. In fact, if we add all the taxes an average citizen pays, the U.S. is among the least taxed country in the Western world.

Furthermore, unlike many other countries, the American tax system is highly skewed towards the wealthy not just in the way the income tax code is written, which limits tax to a maximum percentage of less than 40% no matter what the income, but the code also has a huge number of loopholes for both individuals or families and companies or corporations. In fact, loopholes as well as the tax code itself are so complex that a whole industry of tax consultants, lawyers, public accountants, and advisers are required to assure satisfaction of the tax codes or laws.

The number of tax loopholes and special provisions is huge and many of them allow huge incomes and revenues to be untaxed. For example, oil depletion allowances and other provisions permit huge and very profitable oil companies to evade tax payments. There are similar provisions for large industrial farmers who among other things may get a reward for not growing a crop. There are similar tax exemptions for all kinds of other activities, including even counter-incentive tax exemptions that reward outsourcing and some foreign investments.

Overall, the U.S. tax regime is not only very complex and inefficient but it also encourages and allows tax evasion while wasting huge amounts of time and labor through its complexity, laxity, and encouragement of fraud and evasion. A simpler pro-productivity and fairer taxation system could resolve many of America's economic, trade, and even social problems, and should be a priority for government.

3.1.2 New Approach to Capitalism and Free Markets[14]

Private equity financing of acquisitions has become very popular and now encompasses significant numbers of acquisitions of companies in the U.S. and Europe. The purchases by private equity firms are usually highly leveraged using debt financing. The private equity firms usually use the purchased firms as collateral responsible for servicing the debt. As leverage in financing is usually very large, there is significant risk of failure. The losers are often investors in the firm and its employees if the deal fails. This form of financing acquisitions is attractive in many cases as the cost of borrowing or interest cannot be deducted from tax liabilities in America and some European countries. Another advantage of this method of acquisition is that as a privately owned company, it no longer has the same reporting requirements. Private equity firms now

---

14 Monks, John, "Europe Should Not Give in to Casino Capitalists", *Financial Times*, January 4, 2007.

own large numbers of firms in America, the U.S. and elsewhere, mainly in Europe.

In fact, private equity, venture capital, and similar firms have become a major investment vehicle for wealthy investors who want to limit their exposure and effective wealth management. These new investment vehicles have become very popular and not only attract a growing number of investors, but also companies who need financing to start, grow or expand their business. The advantage of good professional management is counter-balanced by the lack of liquidity.

As noted by John Makis, this approach can really be called "Casino Capitalism" where investors gamble fortunes on shares in major acquisitions. This usually involves purchase of companies which are in financial or management trouble and need a large inflow of cash to grow, survive or diversity.

Private equity firms will usually acquire controlling interests and the power to change management and with this the strategy and operations of the acquired company. They may also try to merge acquired companies. This can be done more efficiently than acquisition of one company by another.

Artificially low interest rates only fuel economic bubbles. When change happens, it must be recognized and timely, effective action taken. It cannot and should not be ignored even if it requires an adjustment of accepted principles. Now that derivatives and other financial tools are used for leveraging, government policymakers, financial institutions, and regulators must recognize the fact that there is a different and increasingly dangerous scale in place for financial transactions which are amplified by electronic and other automated systems. Growth by government stimulation therefore has a magnified and more immediate effect on markets and the economy. We urgently need regulation of derivative trades as well as more instantaneous regulatory reaction; this not only to prevent or discourage abusive risk, but also help ordinary investors from misjudging the magnitude of and exposure to risk. Markets and particularly derivative markets offer inordinate and often new opportunities for manipulation and undermining of investor confidence and reliance on the fairness of the markets or gulf coasts.

3.1.3 AMERICAN LOLLIPOP ECONOMICS

In spring of 2008 at the height of the large sub-prime caused economic crisis in America, the Bush administration with Congressional support devised a scheme for economic revival based largely on the issuance of $250 cash "economic stimulant" payments to citizens who reported net incomes below some level for the year 2007 (up to about $150,000 for a family). Obviously most recipients of this windfall costing an estimated $150 billion to the U.S. Treasury spent this money on wild shopping sprees. While some of it was spent for food, credit card debt reduction, and other essentials, most according to some surveys ended up being spent for toys, clothing, and non-essentials, consisting largely of imported goods.

In other words, the money became an export stimulant for China and other exporting countries, further increasing American foreign debt instead of improving the American economy. This action neither improved the American economy nor the living standards of poor Americans severely damaged by the sub-prime crisis. It had essentially a zero effect on home foreclosures, loss of jobs, and standard of living of the poorest Americans. It was in fact not only a political ploy but a hypocritical attempt to mollify severely damaged suffering people by handing them what amounted to the equivalent of a lollipop given to a starving person.

People needed jobs and incomes and protection from unscrupulous lenders or banks, retailers, and service providers and not a miniscule handout or feel good gesture. In other words, this was really a public relations scam by a desperate government whose "experts" claimed that the lack of consumption was the root problem of the American economy.

For years, certain economists claimed, wrongfully, that as consumption constituted the bulk of the U.S. economy, driving up consumption to higher levels would cure the basic economic problems, such as huge deficits, unemployment, falling production and export, rising foreign trade deficits, and a declining share of the world's economy and market. They did not recognize or chose to ignore the fundamental deficiencies of the American economy with spending out of control, output declining, and America's major asset, its human capital greatly discouraged and disappointed. The leadership did not or chose not to recognize the fundamental faults of the system and that America urgently needed a new dawn, a new economic, strategic, and management approach which would restructure priorities and reorganize America's huge and very competent assets.

There are solutions to America's problems which will also assist the reemergence of Free Market Capitalism and democratic principles as efficient approaches or guidelines for growing prosperity, equality, and rising standards of living in a free democratic environment which is able to eliminate poverty, hunger, sickness, and want, with mutual respect in freedom and equality.

The concept of "too big to fail" used to justify government bailout of banks, insurance companies, and later two of the large automakers set an unacceptable precedence. While some, such as the GM/Chrysler bailout saved tens of thousands of jobs, the same is not clearly the result of the AIG and other bank/financial institution bailouts. All it did in most cases was to save the jobs and obscene compensation (or bonuses) of senior executives of these companies. In fact, the bank/financial services bailouts were supposed to reduce or reverse the terrible costs and effects of the sub-prime mortgage crisis, but they did not and even now in 2010/11 the housing crises and unemployment problems continue.

3.2 American Corporate Welfare

The economic crisis of 2008 has brought many companies in America to their knees. First the financial services and self-serving institutions, including banks, private equity, insurance, and others, clambered for federal government assistance and bail out claiming that the American and probably world economy would suffer or collapse unless the taxpayers stepped in and saved them from collapse resulting largely from excessive risks taken, bad management, and sometimes outright corruption. Hardly had the government stepped into this breach with hundreds of billions of dollars when the big three U.S. automakers ran to Washington demanding $25b of bail out money to top up the $25b already authorized to help them modernize their plants.

The claim was that if they were not to survive the economic crisis, millions of jobs would be lost. These included in addition to the 2-250,000 direct employees (down from over half a million just a few years ago), and 1-2 million working for suppliers and others. The assumption was apparently that if the big three were to go under Americans would no longer make or buy automobiles, while recent history shows that in fact foreign automakers are doing quite well manufacturing cars in America under similar union rules and conditions and are able to produce high quality cars at very reasonable costs.

There is an urgent need for corporate oversight and involvement of shareholders in major decisions as well as in executive compensation, including bonus allocations. These decisions are too important to be left to the sole discretion of executives and boards which are often appointed or selected by management. The reasons are often found to be self-serving and opportunistic instead of having the corporations, its owners (shareholder's) and worker's primary interests in mind. Big bailouts did set a precedence which could justify many other companies or industries to demand government assistance of a bailout as well.

In fact, it is curious that now a year or two after the Big Two (GM and Chrysler) bailout, the American automakers are able to produce better, more fuel efficient cars than ever before. Ford led the way and without any bailout or government aid was able to turn the company around, produce better, less expensive and more desirable cars. Similarly, GM was able and encouraged to come out with an all-electric car as well as other desirable economically priced cars.

It is curious that it took a crisis to have American automakers turn around and produce better and more desirable cars. Much of it appears to be the result of massive shakeups of management and workers who finally recognized that the "Good Old Days" if inefficiency and back scratching was over and that the public and market place demanded better products, more efficiently produced and marketed, and more responsive to the user's needs and not the marketing guru's imagination.

Even though modern corporate management systems were largely developed in America, it was Japan, other East Asian, and European manufacturers who used these systems efficiently. It is curious that some of America's most effective and imaginative management gurus such as Dr. Deming found most ready and effective introduction of their theories and methods not in the good old America but abroad in countries such as Japan, Korea, and later Europe.

At the same time, notwithstanding the decline of U.S. manufacturing and industry, corporate greed continued to escalate with corporate pay and bonuses reaching ever more obscene levels, this unlike much more successful foreign corporations which introduced strict executive reward and remuneration rules.[15] While strict reward ratios were defined in Germany, Japan, Korea, etc. which limited the executive pay, etc. to 20 times that of an average professional employee (say, engineer) not only

---

15   Frankel, E. G., "Mitsui Reward Scheme", The 20-1 Rule of Senior Corporate Remuneration and "Limits on Corporate Pay", internal MIT report.

obscene levels but were also based not on the individual's performance or contribution, but on the overall outcome. Furthermore, reward schemes were never balanced by penalty schemes and which executives would lose or have to return rewards if results were failures. In other words, executive pay or reward was an 'if we win', 'I win', 'if we lose', 'you lose' philosophy.

3.2.1 INSTITUTIONAL BUSINESS

Public institutions in health care, education, and law enforcement are increasingly managed or run by private for-profit businesses in America. Not only do we have for-profit run prisons or hospitals, but increasingly also schools, security, fire prevention, and security services are more and more business ventures. Even during wars of national importance, security logistics and other services are increasingly run by private for-profit companies.

In fact, in recent wars such as the one in Iraq and possibly also Afghanistan, private security personnel probably outnumbered uniformed military personnel. America is the only country that uses so much private sector security services, and there are really important questions about the cost, reliability, loyalty, and effectiveness of this approach. Such services performed primarily with an objective of maximizing profitability introduce real conflicts of interest. Yet increasingly other institutions such as prison services, health care facilities, educational institutions, and more are delegated or contracted out to private profit making enterprises. In fact, such services now employ more people that traditional government departments and agencies in most parts of the country.

In many parts of the country are major differences in the amount of money available for school financing. For example, in the Boston area, some rich suburbs are able to budget and spend 2.5-3.2 times as much per primary, middle, and high school student as other parts of the greater Boston area. As an example, this means that one section of the great metropolitan area may have budgets of over $15,000 per student, while others as little as $4,800. Obviously the amount of funding greatly affects the quality of education, facilities, libraries, and more.

The problem is made even more acute as parental and other outside help in poor neighborhoods with high degrees of near illiteracy or lack of knowledge of English, parental, and other home help for students is practically non-existent, while with richer, more educated populations there is usually a lot of home and other after school hour assistance available. In fact, these examples became a major driving force for the revival of American auto manufacturing and hopefully will similarly help is revive other sectors of our manufacturing industry, such as food, textile, electronic, electrical, office equipment, and appliances.

3.3 America's Energy Greed

American per capita consumption of energy is unreasonably high and on average more than four times the world average. Its petroleum consumption is even higher. It consumes nearly a quarter of the world's demand of oil, with only 5% of the world's population. At the same time, its leaders have refused to make hard decisions that could alleviate the situation, both on the domestic demand and supply side. They have been unwilling to induce a reduction in demand by large tax increases or legal limits on efficiency while at the same time continuing prohibition on drilling for additional oil supplies both onshore and offshore, even though most of such developments could be performed in an environmentally safe manner. Similarly, no new refineries were constructed in America in nearly 30 years which makes America increasingly dependent on refined product imports as well.

The problem is further complicated with different gasoline quality specifications mandated by various state jurisdictions. American ethanol use policies are similarly counterincentive. Ethanol use is mandated and its production mainly from corn highly subsidized. Its production actually consumes more energy than it provides and the policy has had a huge negative impact on corn and other food grain supply and market prices, causing worldwide escalation of fuel costs and availability.

American energy policy has been largely non-existent or ludicrously incompetent for decades. In fact, there really is no such thing as energy policy, certainly not one aimed at reducing energy and particularly oil and gasoline consumption, as well as development of efficient alternative energy sources. Simply talking of energy independence as an economic goal only encourages suppliers to restrict production as well as investment in added sources of supply. The reality of the weak and weakening dollar is another issue driving up the price of oil and other energy sources, without much economic benefit to the American economy.

It could be justified as a strategy for export competitiveness and promotion but America is no longer the large manufacturing, mining, and agricultural supply colossus of the past who would benefit from a weak dollar. American manufacturing in particular is a pale shadow of its past, and the resulting benefits of a more competitive manufacturing industry are therefore minor.

American energy policy includes a large Strategic Petroleum Reserve (SPR) which was supposed to help it as a strategic asset but could also serve to resist large-scale market manipulations. Yet it is apparently only used to satisfy the first objective and has so far not been used to counter temporary market manipulations. In fact, the management of the SPR often enhances or supports the unjustified large-scale price escalation of oil as its management continues purchases no matter what the price of oil. The SPR contains 60-90 days of U.S. imported oil consumption and if properly managed could serve as an effective tool to counter market manipulations.

While many countries are aggressively pursuing alternative (usually renewable) energy developments such as wind energy which supplies over 20% of Denmark's electric power, and Germany, Spain, and others who produce a somewhat smaller percentage by wind power, America is flailing about and has as yet to develop large-scale introduction of wind and solar energy among others. Narrow local objections to possible visual "pollution" such as in the Nantucket offshore wind farms are some of the examples. As noted, no new refinery has been built in 30 years in the U.S., again this largely because of local objections to major industrial complex developments. America wants cheap gas and energy in general as well as a clean environment, but Americans do not want to pay the price of having clean energy generating or modern refining facilities in their backyards. In other words, they want to have their cake and eat it too; cheap clean energy at no cost or inconvenience to them. Let others suffer unsightly refineries, wind farms, and solar energy arrays as long as we Americans get cheap, abundant, clean energy.

Obviously, this argument does not and never really did hold, but Americans for long as the world's premier economy and power were able to impose their preferences. The future, I am afraid, will be different and the U.S. and its people will have to assume a fair share of the burden required to assure delivery of affordable and hopefully cleaner energy in future. This not only involves putting up energy conversion and generating facilities in our backyards, but also new developments such as more offshore drilling in U.S. waters, oil and gas production in the Anwar reserve in Alaska, oil shale mining and oil extraction in the

U.S. Midwest, large solar arrays and wind farms, industrial scale algae production for oil extraction, large-scale agricultural waste collection and fuel extraction, geothermal energy production in the Midwest (Yellowstone National Park), Western U.S., and Hawaii, space solar energy collectors and transmitters, and many more.

All have the potential of reducing America's dependence on oil imports and provide for potentially cleaner energy use and conversion. But all of these, as well as clean coal and nuclear power generation, using mainly domestic resources, extract a price from the American public. The huge escalation in the price of oil in the first half of 2008 at a time when there was no recognizable shortage in supply shows how much oil importers both East and West have become captive to an increasingly irrational, manipulated, and also politically motivated market.

America has been hesitant to develop new sources of oil and gas as well as large-scale production of alternative energy sources. The time has come for a radical change in strategy which invariably will lead to less dependence and ultimately independence of foreign oil imports. Road transport efficiency standards should be tightened with requirements of an average of at least 35 mpg for passenger cars over the short run and 40 mpg over 8-10 years. All-electric drive cars should be marketed for city and commuting purposes which by the way comprises the bulk of vehicle usage in the U.S. The SPR should be used not just as a static emergency reserve but as a dynamic market countering tool to impede speculation in the market.

Large-scale development of new petroleum wells offshore in Alaska and reworked established fields should be encouraged. In parallel, clear coal, carbon sequestration and capture technology should be improved. There are similarly opportunities to reduce aviation fuel consumption by improving both airport and air traffic aircraft control. Most importantly, public transportation must be greatly expanded and improved in quality, accessibility, and service. The average West European or Japanese uses public transport three times more often than his American counterpart in terms of miles traveled and four times as much in terms of trips made.

There is a need to redesign America's freight and passenger transport system. Inland water and coastal shipping consume about a quarter as much fuel and about one-tenth as much as trucks per ton mile. Yet coastal shipping is practically non-existent in the U.S., largely because of the requirements of the long outdated Jones Act of 1936 which requires cabotage (coastal) domestic trade to be carried only on U.S. flag, U.S. built, U.S. manned, and U.S. owned vessels. With prohibitive American shipbuilding costs, very few coastal vessels have been and are being built.

American hub and spoke distribution systems also need to be reevaluated to assure energy use efficiency. These systems were all designed when gas or diesel fuel cost less than one to two dollars per gallon. Also the American power grid requires reevaluation and more efficient management which assure that power inputs are assigned to most efficient plants or excess capacity available. In general, most legislators' suggestions dealing with high oil prices and energy costs were and are useless or made little sense. They did not deal with the fundamental problems and were usually short term. Summer petroleum tax holidays, windfall profit taxes on oil companies, and so on are measures with little if any effect on the fundamental problem. America's Energy Greed (Figure 2) has continued undiminished over the last 25 years notwithstanding all the ominous signs of economic and environmental impacts or costs.

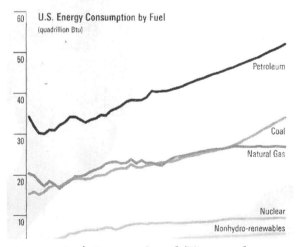

Figure 2: America's Energy Greed (Time scale: 1990-2010)

Similarly, all the pious public announcements and goals for energy conservation and reduction of greenhouse gas emissions such as President Bush's goal of Twenty in Ten decreasing gasoline consumption by 20%

in ten years or by 2017 with 15% from bio-fuels and 5% from better car efficiency is already being questioned, largely because the economic viability of large-scale bio-fuel production and use is increasingly in doubt. Also Congress called for 25% of the nation's energy to be supplied from renewable sources by 2025 (7% in 2007), yet this too is doubtful. At the same time, there are efforts under way to improve our environment by developing cleaner, readily accessible fuels such as coal to gas conversion, solar thermal electric power, efficient geothermal energy extraction, and more.

Geothermal energy generation as noted by Davis and Lema[16] takes a long time to develop and requires huge capital outlays, but once in place supplies reliable energy at little if any cost for an indefinite period of time. There are many attractive sites for geothermal energy developments in Indonesia (Bedugal, Bali), in the U.S. in locations such as Yellowstone National Park, in South Italy, Central Mediterranean, Hawaii, and many more. There are also huge submerged geothermal resources in the Mediterranean between Sicily and Tunisia, with underwater geothermal effluents of enormous capacity; large enough in fact to supply all of Europe's power needs indefinitely. Unfortunately, these huge vents are at depths of 2-3000 meters which will require large-scale technology developments to harness this energy.

Investments into renewable energy worldwide have grown from $80b in 2005 and $100b in 2006 to over $132b in 2007, according to the United Nations Environmental Program (UNEP). Ethanol, the most common bio-mass originated fuel which is largely produced from corn, sugar cane, and other food grains or products will in future hopefully be mainly produced from agricultural waste, wild grasses, wood waste, and more materials not parts of the normal food chain.

In parallel, there are many developments in energy conversion technology which should permit radical (10-30%) reduction in fuel consumption. These and the trends towards smaller, lighter, more fuel efficient cars (hybrid, electric drive, etc.) should allow us to not just reduce the rate of increase in gasoline consumption but actually reverse the trend and start a decline which should bring us back to 1990 levels within 10 years.

America is and always has been a resource rich nation. But unlike many others, it has and is using its riches largely to satisfy a voracious

---

16   Davis, Ed and Lema, Karen, "Pricey Oil Making Geothermal Projects More Attractive", International Herald Tribune, June 20, 2008.

appetite for excess consumption and not mainly to enhance its trade. As the world's third largest producer of oil now and first or second largest producer in the past, it should have been able to develop a largely self-sufficient economy in terms of oil. In addition, the country has one of the largest reserves of coal, huge reserves of oil shale, abundant hydropower potentials, as well as geothermal and other energy sources. Yet, with all these riches, the country has become increasingly dependent on oil imports which now constitute more than 58% of domestic consumption and an unjustified 25% of world oil consumption of about 83-84 million barrels per day.

If Americans were to consume as much oil per capita as say people in equally rich countries such as Germany or Japan, not only would the country not require any oil imports but it would actually be able to export some. Furthermore, such a change would reduce the foreign trade deficit significantly. American fuel taxes have been the lowest among developed oil importing countries for a long time. It is curious that American consumers object to higher taxation or at least that is what our politicians assume, but hardly change their consumption when large price increases are imposed by the market or exporters. It seems that a $2.00 per gallon or so fuel surcharge or tax would probably stabilize the fuel market in America, and continue the, albeit initially small, move towards conservation. At the same time, it would provide the government with additional revenues of more than $500 billion per year which could be used to upgrade our road infrastructure, automobile technology, alternative fuel distribution systems, public transport systems, and more. Such a more may bring American road transport fuel consumption closer to that of other developed countries, while allowing America to rebuild its land transport infrastructure so as to be able to achieve efficiencies and qualities of service comparably to those in Western Europe, Japan, and others.

3.3.1 American Oil Production

Although the high price of oil has encouraged a bevy of secondary production in formerly abandoned fields in America, most of the new recoverable reserves of oil are expected to become available offshore. Forty-five billion barrels of oil are estimated to be recoverable in the U.S. Gulf of Mexico, though an increasing percentage of that production is expected in deep (1000'-7500') or ultra deep (7500' +) waters. Much of these new production developments will require use of Floating

Production Storage and Offloading (FPSO) units. There are also potentially offshore prospects on the Southern Atlantic East and some parts of the U.S. West Coast which added to ANWAR in Alaska may offer reserves of more than 65 billion barrels or the equivalent of 15 years of oil imports at current (2007) levels.

These offshore developments require new technical approaches which increasingly advise the use of floating versus fixed production structures, particularly for use in hurricane prone areas. Following the extensive experience of Petrobras with FPSOs served by shuttle tankers, this approach is now considered to provide safer, more reliable, and cost effective transportation for deep water produced crude oil than pipeline transport.

The U.S. Gulf of Mexico produces now (2008) about 27% of America's domestic oil production on 43 million acres leased. It is expected that new deeper water leases will add as much as 1 million barrels per day of new production by 2016. At the same time, output from existing Gulf of Mexico offshore wells may fall by as much as 500,000 barrels per day, for a net increase of 500,000 barrels per day.

In parallel, various other developments are underway. American oil shale and Canadian tar sand oil extraction has been expanded, with the projected oil production of 2 million barrels per day from Canadian tar sands by 2015. Altogether America alone is expected to attain production levels of 10-11 million barrels per day by 2015 and maintain this output for 10-20 years, with at least 1 million barrels per day coming from secondary production from previously abandoned wells.

3.3.2 Carbon Trading as an Environmental Benefit and Economic Boom

Carbon trading is expected to become a major tool for emissions control as envisioned by the Kyoto Protocol. In fact, it may become a very important market, providing a most important incentive for improvement in air quality a major influencing factor in oil and coal trades and thereby the price of electric power and more, as noted by Harvey and Kirchgaessner[17]. It may in fact become a major factor in the global economy and may affect the development of combustion and emission reduction technology.

The largest emitter of CO_2 in 2007 was China with 24% of world

---

17 Harvey, Fiona and Kirchgaessner, Stephanie, "Carbon Trading", Financial Times, June 18, 2008.

total, followed by the U.S. with 21%, the EU15 with 12%, India 8%, Russia 6%, and the rest of the world .29%. Yet on a per capita basis in tons per capita of CO_2, the U.S. emits over 19.4 tons/person, Russia 11.8 tons/person, EU15 8.2 tons/person, China 5.0 tons/person, and India just under 2 tons/person as per person.[18]

Global carbon trading monitored by the World Bank Carbon Finance Unit has grown from $10b in 2005 to over $62.3b in 2007. This has therefore become a very important market. Yet there are many who feel that a carbon tax system would be preferable to such a trading system. There is a wide consensus though that it is essential to bring down emissions and carbon trading permits a trade off between expensive and lower cost emission reduction. A market-based trading system permits more efficient trade-offs, yet many feel that it involves mostly the producers and not the consumers and general public. In any case, there is agreement that long-term targets and policies are essential. While the U.S. did not participate in the Kyoto Protocol provisions which must be renewed in 2012, it is expected that a new U.S. administration in 2009 will join in the general clean air efforts and invest in clean energy to counter pollution. It is likely that carbon trading will be found to be the most efficient and fair mechanism to reduce global pollution.

Such a cap and trade system for CO_2 based on carbon credits issued by the UN appears to be the direction in which we will go. In this, carbon quotas are issued and permits to emit more must be bought as additional carbon permits. Carbon credits obviously vary in price dependent on the cost of reducing emissions. As a result, for example, EU-ETS credits are much more expensive than say low cost developing country credits. The world is waiting for American participation in this global carbon market which some such as "Point Carbon", a carbon market analysis group, estimated will grow to a $3 trillion market.

There will be a continued discussion if taxing carbon emissions is more effective than carbon trading, in reducing carbon emissions which most scientists agree must be reduced by 50% from current levels if the greenhouse effects are to be reversed. Carbon taxes would be hard to collect and unpopular as they affect all energy consumers, while carbon trading affects only companies and is easier to organize and manage. But something must be done. An obvious issue is that developing countries including India and China feel that they have in the past contributed very little emissions and should as a result not be required

---

18   Netherland Environmental Assessment Agency, 2008.

to reduce emissions by the same percentage as big polluters among the industrialized nations such as the U.S. and Europe which contributed to the bulk of the atmospheric pollutants. The argument is fair and just and must be considered.

Most importantly, America which actually introduced some carbon trading years ago should join the world carbon trading market, accept the current Kyoto Protocol, and work with the UN on developing another updated carbon trading market mechanism and emission reduction standards which are fair in terms of their socio-economic impact.

A new issue[19] is the imposition of carbon taxes on imports from other countries. These taxes would be based on the emissions during their manufacture. Proponents of these taxes that without them would encourage "carbon leakage" as companies transfer their polluting industries to countries with no or lesser air quality regulation. Such carbon border taxes introduce a new challenge to the World Trade Organization (WTO). At the same time, there would be a huge impact on U.S. exports to the EU if it were to impose such taxes to compensate for the lack of U.S. Kyoto Protocol acceptance. The issue is very complex as newly developing countries such as China and India would invariably argue the case of comparative historic emission developments.

Furthermore, modern outsourcing and supply chains may make it very difficult to determine carbon debits based on how much of a product is produced or assembled in a particular country. A global uniform carbon debit system would have to be developed and accepted for such a system to work. For the time being, carbon taxes imposed only by some countries will simply skew competitiveness in international trade and foster further outsourcing to low labor cost and carbon tax environments.

3.3.3 American Alternative Energy Developments and Acceptance

America, while at the forefront of most alternative and usually renewable energy sources, lags far behind other nations in their adoption and use. While several European nations produce 10-20% of their electricity from wind power, and France produces over 70% of its electric power using nuclear reactors, the U.S. produces just a few percent of its electricity using wind power, and just fewer than 30% for nuclear, hydro,

---

19 Beattie, Alan, "Green Barricade", Trade Faces a New Test as Carbon Taxes Go Global", Financial Times, January 24, 2008.

and other non-fossil fuel using power plants. This notwithstanding that America has and in many cases developed the most advanced nuclear, hydro, wind, wave, geothermal, and photovoltaic solar energy conversion technologies. The reasons are that in America energy use, generating technology and location of electric generating capacity is highly politicized with little consideration for either the environment or economics. True, most Americans are for clean, cheap, and readily available abundant energy, but are not willing to make any sacrifices, pay the real cost of power delivery, and are unwilling to accept any type of industrial structure they consider esthetically unattractive in their neighborhood. In other words, they want abundant, cheap, clean energy but are unwilling to pay the real costs of its delivery. This has become a major problem for America and a prime political issue which most leaders are unwilling to tackle. However, tackle they must, and it is curious to note the flip-flopping of the 2008 Presidential candidates on this issue.

Americans are not just spoiled by the availability of abundant cheap energy but also by a political system which permits any group of citizens to override the public interest if they can show even the slightest damage to their freedom of choice, environment or other consideration. They are used to unlimited access to energy of all kinds and the freedom to choose the most convenient and/or cheapest without consideration of the local, common or general good. This has had a negative energy waste, pollution, and introduction as well as use of alternative, renewable energy.

Al Gore[20] declared at an energy conference in Washington that the future of human civilization is at stake unless we rely more or even nearly exclusively on clean energy for electricity generation within 10 years or by 2018. America's national security as well as the comforts of its citizens will be at risk unless such transition is achieved by then. Carbon free power generation is not only achievable but will also be affordable if we put our true political will behind such transformation.

America's reliance on foreign oil and increasing impacts of greenhouse gases make America politically and economically highly vulnerable. He proposed taxes on CO_2 emissions and a reduction of payroll taxes. Solar, wind, wave, geothermal, hydro, and other natural energy sources are not only abundant but increasingly more economic to

---

20 Stout, David, "Gore Urges US to Use Clean Fuel by 2018", Herald Tribune, July 18, 2008.

generate, a process which would not only assure a more environmentally clean economy but an America which would no longer depend on borrowing funds from China and others to pay for oil and gas imports from the Middle East and other increasingly unreliable suppliers.

There are many exciting developments in energy storage and fuels. A123 Systems of Watertown, Massachusetts, USA developed a new approach and designed a compact high capacity battery. They use extremely thin layers of nano-phosphate which makes their batteries both small and quickly chargeable. The system should become available as a conversion plug-in or in new cars within a few years.

Amgris of Emeryville developed a new type of bio-diesel much more efficient, cheaper to produce, and transport and cleaner burning than largely corn-based ethanol. The latter as known also requires nearly as much energy to produce than it provides, making it economically and environmentally less attractive. In fact, developments of bio-fuels continue to advance both in economic as well as environmental impact terms and the use of bio-fuels is expected therefore to continue to advance globally.

4.0 Fixing America's Economic, Social, and Stragegic Problems

It is increasingly evident that America has to make radical changes in its economy, social systems, and strategic approaches to survive as a super power and world leader. As a nation, it is now broke and not only owes more at home and abroad than any nation in history, but there are also few signs of how it could or would turn its economy around to correct this problem, reduce its indebtedness, pay for its expenses, maintain living standards and conditions, as well as the various obligations it assumed or is expected to fulfill worldwide.

It appears that America will not be able to continue as a super power, over-spender, protector of other nations, and leader in science, technology, military power, and beacon of free market economic democracy without some radical changes in its domestic policies and methods. Apart from downplaying consumerism and prestige or show off there are many other things that must be done. We need more and stricter regulations, fairer tax rates, higher consumption taxes, particularly for energy, liquor, tobacco, and recreational drugs.

We have to improve our education, health care, and law enforcement systems, all of which lag behind those of many other countries, notwithstanding the fact that we spend more than anyone on these as a percentage of our GDP. We will have to work more years and hours, in line with increased life expectancy. We will have to make politicians more responsive to the electorate and reduce the influence of special interests.

In other words, we will have to return to our roots and the principles of our founding fathers and the builders of this country. Consumption as an economic driving force is wrong. Consumption must be justified by need and not economic policy. We not only owe two trillions of dollars, but many of our essential social support systems, such as Social Security, are also not sustainable and in essence will be bankrupt before long. Yet, we undertake unnecessary and costly adventures such as the wars in Iraq and Afghanistan, waste on major inefficiencies in health care, education, and law enforcement, yet effort to refrain from maintaining our infrastructure are ineffective in our disaster response, and allow our financial and other systems to bypass necessary regulation and rules to protect the public.

We allow huge bonuses for gamblers in banking who risk investor's or public funds, yet we do not require the same people to participate in or make good losses when their gambles do not work out. Solutions to these shortcomings and problems are not easy, but there are ways we could at least correct some, if not all, these problems.

The suggestions or plans presented here may not be popular and will penalize a few who have been able to ride the system, but they are designed to right our ship of state and not just correct current ills but also put it on a long-term and firm, yet just, footing. To start, we have to recognize that we spend more on education, health care, and law enforcement than anyone else in per capita GDP terms, yet get significantly less for our money than others.

1. Taking education as one example, we not only spend more money but also more time educating our people. Americans on average spend 30% more years before joining the work force than most people in other developed countries; this is largely because in the U.S. 72% of all attend college which is 50% higher than the number of college (tertiary) education attendees in other developed countries. In most other developed countries, such as Germany, Japan, UK, etc., less than 50% of high school graduates continue into university or college, with the rest usually spending a year or less in vocational or job training. In America, most high school graduates continue schooling in a college with a majority enrolled in liberal arts colleges or remedial high schools where they learn what they should have learned in high school. Most of these then spend 4 years of their lives without any meaningful job or professional education. As a result, the average age at which people start a professional career or job is 3-4 years older than in most other developed countries. Furthermore, fewer opt for value output careers, with most going into service types of jobs. The implications of this are serious as we not only lose 4 years or more of productive work, but also contributions to Social Security, health care, and taxes, non-repaid student loans, and more. In other words, the fact that 50% more school leavers in the U.S. spend or waste an additional 4 years in remedial high school (liberal arts college) education cost as:

1. Loss of 10% of the lifetime professional output of the working life of our workers.
2. Hundreds of thousands of dollars in educational expenses.
3. Loss of Social Security, etc. contributions by millions of people who join the work force 4 years later, but retire with full benefits at normal retirement age.

A rough calculation of the economic impact of liberal arts or remedial high-school phenomena shows that it costs us about $500 billion a year, on top of the losses in Social Security and health care cost contributions. In fact, rough calculations show that Social Security would and could be financially much more solid than without these contributions.

The total lifetime man hours lost is about 10%. Therefore, total national economic output could increase by 5% much if working life of the 50% of people who spent these 4 years of working life on remedial high school education would join the workforce at age 19 instead of 22 or 23.

Similarly, with life expectancy now of nearly 80 years, official retirement age should be raised to at least 68 as it is in many developed countries now. The combination of a 10% increase in working years of 5% of the population and increase in the retirement age to 68 would go a long way in making Social Security and health care financially viable again. The liberal arts colleges should be converted into professional training schools which provide both full time training for school leavers as well as continue education for the general workforce who should be required to return to school for an 8-10 week mandatory period every 4 years (paid for by employers) for most skills or professions as done in many countries to assure that people remain up to date professionally, while on their employer's payroll. Only this way will we be able to assure that we remain competitive. Employers would be given tax incentives for funding employee retraining.

There is an urgent need to overhaul our primary, secondary, and tertiary educational systems. Most importantly, we will have to make primary education more equitable by financing it centrally as in most countries instead of relying on local school financing which automatically discriminates against children in poor states and neighborhoods which actually need more and better support than children in richer neighborhoods who get a lot of parental and other support from their surroundings. Again, most developed countries finance their school systems nationally and provide central supervision, quality control, and other support.

Another important issue is school budget allocation. Here again American schools spend an inordinate percentage of their budgets on prestige sports like football which very few of their students play. In fact, some schools spend more on their prestige sports than all other sport activities combined, benefiting a very small percentage of their students. We need more support and encouragement of participating sport as any student can benefit from and enjoy, not just for fairness but also health reasons.

To assure improvements and greater effectiveness of professional education, there is also an urgent need to redefine qualification and licensing requirements. For example, the U.S. is unique in the college training of nurses and to some degree teachers. Professionals, like nurses, need effective skill training and retraining. Changes in and use of advanced technology now introduce many new demands and skill/knowledge requirements for professionals such as nurses, medical assistants, facility operators, and more.

Similarly, information management has become much more technical and professionals such as nurses, first aid personnel, and others need to know how to deal with. Much of the troublesome paperwork imposed by health care and malpractice insurers will have to be automated and simplified before the paper avalanche buries our health care system.

Additionally, medical malpractice insurance should be relocated and put under the supervision of medical professionals, not lawyers, who have only quality not just money and profit as their central interest. Medical boards are much better qualified to judge if malpractice has occurred and should be empowered to punish offenders by license revocation and/or monetary verdicts.

As judges will routinely ask for medical expert witnesses to evaluate malpractice claims, they should be empowered to actually judge the medical results and award damages as well as monetary or professional punishments of doctors. Ambulance chasing has become a very expensive practice. Not only does it add the huge cost of malpractice insurance to our medical costs, but it also forces doctors to use defensive medicine which may not result in the best appropriate and available treatment.

Instead, doctors should be required to fully explain and document the strategy or procedure they want to recommend and use and give patients a full disclosure of it, its requirements, effects, and their experience and success rate using it. Lawyers' and courts' involvement should only be used in cases where a clear, criminal behavior or intent is assumed or discovered. Ready access to and use of information equips us with tools that should allow much more informed decisions by doctors and patients and easy documentation of the rational for and proposed procedure for use of a procedure.

With all information (pre, during, and post procedure) readily available and accessible, independent medical experts are much better qualified to judge malpractice or other immoral or unprofessional treatment. Lawyers and courts, as mentioned, should only be involved if and when professional arbitration boards determine or suspect criminal behavior. The same should also apply to other types of claims of professional misconduct by auditors, builders, carpenters, home improvement workers, and more. It is estimated that such a change would not just reduce the cost of medical, legal, service, home improvement, and other services of 20-30%, but it would also reduce waiting times, waste, and ultimately improve the quality and responsiveness of such services.

The total savings of eliminating much of the legal costs would be as much as 10-20% of the gross value of all such services. Like the savings in medical service cost, these will also be of the order of hundreds of billions of dollars. In most other developed countries, adjudication of malpractice, lack of quality management or other unprofessional behavior is judged and adjudicated by professionals or boards of professionals who are given legal powers to adjudicate the case and impose appropriate punishments and damages. They act with full knowledge of backing by the legal system and can rely on the state to back up their decisions. However, the question often arises of conflict of interest in having a professional board export judging colleagues in the same profession. Experience shows that such board members are usually more concerned with assurance of the quality and reputation of their profession than the performance of a colleague.

4.1 Loss of Technological Leadership

After centuries of rapid technological advances, we now face needs and opportunities for even greater technological advances. While many of these will be new breakthroughs and others will be technologies to meet needs, we never thought we had or recognized before an even greater number will be technological advances or breakthroughs developed to negate or at least reduce the negative effects of earlier technological developments. In fact, more and more of human endeavors will be occupied with solving or diminishing ill effects of earlier human advances or technological developments.

While many of these will try to reverse the impacts of air and water pollution and in general the effects of effluents and wastes generated by modern man, there will be many new technological developments designed to provide for human needs never before envisioned or identified. Science and technology have advanced the human condition in many parts of the world and improved human health, comfort, life expectancy, and opportunity; yet it also caused more disparity in standards of living, greater conflict, and adversity among people.

America was the recognized leader in the development and use of technology in the twentieth century. In fact, technology was the principal locomotive in advancing the American economy and life style to unprecedented levels. America and everything American became the envy of the world and the standard for economic, social, and cultural development.

America reached its pinnacle of technological prowess during and after World War II. Not only was it responsible for the majority of technological breakthroughs in electronics, nuclear technology, structural engineering, transportation, communications, and more but it also developed new medical devices, testing equipment, and more. In parallel, it used this technology to rebuild and advance its power, transport, communications, health care, and other infrastructure. It rebuilt its roads, ports, airports, power plants, hospitals, schools, prisons, telephone, water supply, sewage, and other systems, and then rested on its laurels as priority was given to the space and armaments race with the Soviet Union. Infrastructure development as well as its maintenance took a back seat and it soon became outdated and started deteriorating.

This trend not only continued during the last few decades of the 20th century but engineering and technology developments lost their attraction. Science and services, particularly financial services became the focus of attention and prestige. Curricula, grant programs, research, and course offerings at universities adapted to the new priorities and engineering in all its branches assumed a passé reputation. The result is that today less than a decade into the 21st century America finds itself with an old, outdated, ill-maintained infrastructure, a dearth of capable of engineers and engineering firms, a largely non-competitive manufacturing industry.

4.1.1 AMERICAN TRANSPORT

High gas prices, deteriorating highways, and road congestion may finally convince Americans and their governments to redevelop the nation's railway system, particularly passenger rail, a sector long in the doldrums. Amtrak, the national passenger rail system, is barely coasting along, using outdated rail system and communication infrastructure, rolling stock and stations. There is an urgent need to upgrade America's railroad system, not just because of high gas prices but also to reduce road congestion, greenhouse gases, and even loss of life.

Americans spent about 3.7 billion hours stuck in traffic. Apart from some improvements in the Northeast Corridor from Boston to Washington, rail transport in the U.S. is barely used and has become an anachronism. The rest of the developed world of Europe, Japan, Korea, and more is spending huge amounts and effort on railway systems, developing high speed trains, modern stations, high tech communications and control systems, and efficient reservation and passenger handling systems. Amtrak never reached its projected level of service and improvements were haphazard at best. The Acela and Metro, so-called high speed services on the East Coast corridor, never met their projected goals, partly because of inadequate technology but mostly because of lack of competent infrastructure.

Amtrak is federally funded and received about $1.3b in 2006, about the same as in 1981 compared to $40b for highways and $14b for airlines in 2006, and funding for Amtrak is projected to decline to less than $700 in 2008. In fact, the administration has attempted to null all Amtrak federal subsidies. Most railways in the world are richly supported by governments who recognize their economic contributions. The lack of effective rail service in America is a major factor contributing to the high inter- and intra-urban use of automobiles and the consequent high gasoline consumption, road and highway capacity demand, and air pollution. It is estimated that America could reduce its gasoline or oil demand by 50% or more if an adequate national railway network system and service were provided.

Just improving East Coast rail service to a level where it replaces much of the intercity road transport could save as much as 2 million barrels per day in gasoline consumption, more than the potential output of all new offshore oil wells and ANWAR in Alaska combined, and reduce greenhouse gas emissions to the levels of 1990.[21] The costs of improving the American passenger rail system in the one-third of America east of the Mississippi would be about $80-100b over a 10-year period or only about half of the money spent on highway projects in that region during that period; yet the impact would be tremendous not just in terms of oil or gas consumption and air quality improvements, but also on quality of life, convenience, and mobility.

Congress is considering a $10b project over 4 years to develop high speed, short haul rail corridors which Western European nations so successfully introduced and are operating. The French have a nationwide network of 200 mph TGV trains going north-south and east-west across the country as has Spain, Germany, and Japan. China is planning to spend hundreds of billions of dollars in the development of high-speed passenger rail transport not just between the major East Coast cities from Beijing to Nanjing, Shanghai, and Guanzhou (Canton), but also connecting major cities in the interior and the interior with the Pacific Coast. High speed rail transport not only relieves congested and fuel expensive road transport, but also air travel which is not only equally fuel inefficient but requires increasingly expensive, mainly publicly-funded infrastructure.

4.2   Who is an American?

Although North, Central, and South America form the American continent, inhabitants of the United States of (North) America are commonly referred to us Americans. Others, particularly Spanish speaking people living in the USA, Central or South America, are generally referred to as Latinos. This is quite curious and the identity of the USA is really in question because of it, particularly as Spanish speakers in the country are increasing at a rapid rate and have become the largest group of people and may even become a majority before the end of this century if the trend continues.

America is a nation of immigrants and has quite artificially retained its linguistic and cultural association with Britain, notwithstanding the fact that a small minority of its population descend from British immigrants. Questions therefore arise – what does and should hold this polyglot nation together? – is it historic affiliation or common interest? America received immigrants from over 65 nations and 60%

---

21   Richmond, Peter, "Better Way to Travel", Parade, November 2007.

of its population are born in or descendants of people from only 6 countries. There are several ethnic groupings that dominate in certain parts of the country or locations. Similarly, some people have been here for generations, while others are newcomers or first/second generation Americans. In recent years, immigration has been largely from Latin and Caribbean locations and these people, unlike previous generations of European and Asian immigrants, find it less attractive or necessary to assimilate in both language and customs; this because they usually reside in ethnic neighborhoods and have less incentives to advance and relocate into more typical and mixed neighborhoods.

At the same time, Americans of African descent do become more integrated with the main stream and since the election of the first African American President of the U.S. have finally broken the glass ceiling of political power in America. Equity in economic opportunity continues to escape or diminish, with gaps between worker and manager, uneducated and professional, as well as banking/financial service stars or gamblers and work force growing to irrational and counter-incentive levels.

While in Japan and most other Eastern economies, high earners such as CEOs and large investors usually earn 20-30 times what a mid-level professional or employee does, the multiple in America has grown to an obscene and unsustainable multiple of 50-100 which is not only unjustified but counter-incentive. It not only undermines the social and economic fiber of the society, but also encourages misuse of trust, dishonest dealings, and social unrest, as few accept such rewards as honestly earned. In fact, this type of economic or reward distortion exerts a negative effect on the economy and cultural growth of America and seriously undermines its social and cultural contract.

Americans have always been innovators and originators in a social, technical, and operational sense. However, much of this is dependent on opportunity, equity, and openness. Many of the recent developments, particularly in government and business, are seriously undermining the basic belief of American's and others in the inherent characteristics of America as the land of the free and infinite opportunity. Equity in opportunity has been greatly prostituted or distorted and the land of the free and of great opportunity for all has become the land of the reward for special interests, the dishonest, and speculator. There is a need for a revival of old values and approaches if America is to regain its historic greatness, leadership, and opportunity.

4.3 MILITARY MIGHT ALONE DOES NOT AND CANNOT ASSURE AMERICA'S PROSPERITY

America has grown largely through the ingenuity and hard work of its people, in addition to its huge natural resource endowments and riches. However, in recent years we have started to ignore or misuse both of these historic opportunities. We have become a low productivity, low output society that continues to consume much more than it produces. America used to be a major food, service, and industrial products exporter and largely self-sufficient in all these areas, but no more. Much of our food, manufactured goods, and even services now originate abroad; this not for lack of resources or capacity, but productivity and costs. This dependence on foreign goods and services has and will increasingly affect America's ability to lead in the world and to maintain its living standards.

We have fallen behind many other countries not just in output, efficiency, and costs, but also quality of products and services. In areas in which we ruled supreme no long ago, we have fallen well below the standards, quality, and costs of other countries, including many developing countries. While we may still have and are the dominant military power in the world, our economic prowess and general leadership qualities are increasingly in doubt or outright inferior. This will make it increasingly difficult to sustain world leadership, as our credibility is now frequently questioned.

4.3.1 THE RISE AND FALL OF GREAT POWERS

For thousands of years men had established great empires, with some lasting just a few years and others hundreds of years. In Europe most of the great empires developed around the Mediterranean Sea from the Egyptian, Pharos, Persian, Greek, and later Roman and Ottoman empires. There were similar developments in the Americas and in Central and East Asia.

Those who lasted centuries usually managed to combine military power and domination with economic as well as cultural advances. They often also managed to delegate power to and distribute wealth to some of their vassals. In most cases, their power declined when over-indulgence and over-confidence undermined discipline and principle. These rules continue to apply to these days. Not only did the British, French, Dutch, and other European colonial powers overreach themselves, but Asian powers, such as China, had preceded them.

In the Americas, similarly Central and South American empires, were decimated and defeated when they overreached themselves and often as a result lost their basic support or more importantly the principles which had helped make them great. These lessons apply equally to today. America was built on principles of freedom, equality, and laws. It grew with the arrival of hordes or mainly European and later African immigrants; the former, largely refugees from religion, ethnic or economic persecution, the latter largely by forcible transfer.

Americans society of European descent recognized that basic principles of equality, lawfulness, and equal opportunity were necessary for the development of a just, prosperous, civilized society, though it took it hundreds of years to accept these principles for all. In fact, defeated Indians whose properties and rights were often forcefully taken became an apartheid people, often herded into so-called reservations.

4.4 Who Will Rule the World in the Future?

After centuries of European and American or Western so-called Atlantic nations domination of the world's economy, politics, and strategic or military powers, the global landscape is steadily but surely changing. After all, the recent economic, financial, and military misadventures of the West, particularly America, Asian countries though damaged will emerge with greater strength, a more solid footing, a better economy, and probably a better social, educational, and health care system.

They will also challenge the West or Atlantic nations in science and technology. Asians, particularly East Asians, have a less selfish and self-satisfying culture, good work attitude and ethics, greater frugality, and well developed social systems. As a result, they consume less, put greater emphasis on education, social harmony, and interpersonal relations, all of which result in good productivity and social advances. Even though free market economies have served the West well and have provided incentives for advancing science, technology, medicine, as well as social conditions, it invariably led to personal and social greed, international as well as domestic conflicts, interruptions of social harmony, and corruption, both private and public. The main reasons for these were the lack of understanding of and agreement on the incentives and regulation required to assure honesty and common trust among peoples.

As a result, we have experienced more international and domestic conflicts, notwithstanding the large increase in living standards and personal freedoms in most parts of the world. One reason for this is our inability to decide on the boundaries of social and economic freedoms that assure honesty, decency, and support of the common interests. While many argue that free capitalist markets provide the incentives and initiatives to advance science, technology, finance, medicine, and more, all for the common good, recent experience shows this is be true only if certain moral values, honesty, education, and cultural values are emphasized or required. In fact, some regulation may also be required to remind people of their obligations towards each other, society, and the common good - and not just personal advancement. As people, Westerners, and particularly Americans, have become so enamored with consumption, not just to meet their needs or desires, but also as a sign of status, superiority, and self-indulgence. People in the East, with a much lesser luxurious past and history of human and natural deprivations or shortfalls, are much more oriented towards frugality and less prone to waste in a material, intellectual, and social sense.

This gives the newly developing countries of Asia and South America, such as China, India, and Brazil, major advantages. Their rate of growth and economic development is now a multiple of that of the traditional Western-style economies of Western Europe and North America. As a result, the economic center of the world is rapidly moving from the Mediterranean/Atlantic regions towards the Western Pacific and Indian Ocean areas.

This change has not only economic but also great cultural impact. Christianity and other Abrahamic religions which served as the cultural foundation of Western and Middle Eastern faiths and culture are increasingly being replaced by Eastern religions, faiths or beliefs. Among the most important developments in the reemergence of Confucianism which is a faith with strict moral, intellectual, and social codes or guidelines.

Its reemergence and increasingly important influence played an important role in the rapid advance of East and South East Asian cultural and economic advances; this while Europe and America are facing increasingly difficult internal and international confrontations and discords. The increasingly adversarial relations between Islam and Christian-Judaic groupings are becoming a major destructive force in demolishing the two millennia long dominance of the West.

The demands for critical resources for energy, construction, food, water, and manufacturing will continue in future access to these resources will increasingly based on mutually beneficial trading and other arrangements and not physical domination which, in the nuclear age, is too self-destructive.

4.5 DOES THE WORLD WANT AMERICA TO LEAD?

America assumed global strategic and economic leadership during World War I, and then largely withdrew only to resume the leadership during and after World War II. Yet today nearly 10 years into the 21st century, more and more people and their leaders doubt America's ability and qualifications to lead the world. Much of America's credibility has been lost not only because of its ill-advised military interventions but also its failure to convey confidence in its financial, economic, industrial, social, and political activities. American inventiveness and creativity are still admired, but there is an increasing mistrust of its business practices, economic and trade policies, and socio-political values. America's consumerism, wasteful practices, and lack of effective environmental management are not only unpopular abroad but are considered largely irresponsible and selfish.

In fact, America is widely considered to have lost its way and to flounder about, trying to maintain or regain its leader status. However, many abroad as well as within its own citizens doubt America's ability to continue to lead the world. In fact, unless America changes its selfish consumerism and business practices, much of its principal assets may soon be owned by foreigners or foreign governments. Superior military power may maintain America's leading role for a while, but it also will soon eclipse and lose its importance.

How did we move from being the most productive and efficient country to one which barely surpasses advancing developing nations? Not only has our productivity seriously declined but so has our inventiveness and leadership; this not only in a scientific and technological sense, but also in terms of work habits, organization, and demands for things we do not earn or deserve. There is a real question of morality and concern with our demands for awards and leadership which are difficult to defend.

5.0 Saving America

America's economic, financial, even physical condition is dire now and it has lost much of its global respect as well as influence. While still the largest economy and trader, it is generally considered to be in decline. At the same time, its leaders and much of its population continue to assume that nothing has changed and the country continues on its merry path of waste, spending, and foreign adventures, while it is not only slipping deeper into debt, is losing its strategic prowess and respect. While still feared, America is not taken seriously any more.

Government should stop so-called bail outs and start a really big, focused spending program. Spending unlike bail outs, tax relief, and so-called stimuli produce jobs, develop assets, use material and services, and really prime the economy. Bail outs just keep failed and basically unproductive institutions alive and their executives in unearned luxury they have become used to, and stimuli or tax breaks only provide money to people to buy what they often do not need and benefit foreign producers or are used to reduce people's personal debt which they probably should not have assumed in the first place. The Paulson bail out was nothing but a package to save and reward incompetent, greedy, overpaid, useless financial executives for their greed and for gambling with other people's money, and often losing it.

We must save ourselves from over-indulgence, over-confidence, and lack of meaningful output. In other words, we will have to strengthen our meaningful productive output and stop relying primarily on self-indulgence. As described in my 1998 book on *America's Institutional Dilemma*[22], you cannot have and grow a healthy economy based solely on services, particularly services for them alone. There must be a significant, real productive segment which produces, grows, and manufactures materials and goods for consumption and sale.

We must develop and emerge an economy which has a better balance between government, services, and real productive output. We cannot continue to just use, consume, and meet our own needs, particularly

---

22 Frankel, Ernst G., *"America's Institutional Dilemma"*, Vantage Press, New York, 1998.

as we become more and more dependent on other people's or nations' output and resources. We used to be the world's largest producer of many agricultural goods, minerals, and manufacturers, but no more. This change demands new strategies, approaches and priorities in addition to some sacrifice or at least roll backs which will be suggested later in this book.

America became the wonder of the 20th century. From a distant recently freed British overseas colony, it emerged as the star of freedom for European and Asian immigrants in the 19th century. However, it would take until later in the 20th century for the former black slaves or their descendants to receive full civil rights. In fact, even though black citizens served in the military and elsewhere carried their economic burden, they were discriminated against.

Since then, major questions are being raised about immigration, particularly as Latin heritage citizens and residents are growing at an increasing rate and now constitute the most rapidly growing group of citizens now. In fact, Spanish has become a true second language in many parts of the country. At the same time, radical changes in the economic structure of the country have reduced availability of low level manufacturing and agricultural jobs, the traditional stepping stones for new immigrants.

America is facing many new issues and problems, some resulting from changes in the world at large, nature, technological, and economic developments, others self-induced and the result of insensitivity, greed, ignorance or prejudice. Americans continue to be arrogant, self-confident, and in many cases domineering even when they know and often admit that past superiority or leadership is no more.

It is evident to most that America no longer leads in many fields as it once did. We lag far behind many countries in the quality of our infrastructure from high-speed trains, efficient (electric, water, communication, sewage, etc.) distribution systems, modern grid, air control systems, ports, airports, and more. However, listening to our leaders, politicians, newscasters, and others, we continue to be told daily that we are the best, the richest, the most productive, powerful, and smartest; this when many of us know this is no longer true.

Infrastructure construction and maintenance jobs done elsewhere in hours or weeks, take weeks, months or years here. Our school children lag those in many other countries, not just in math and science but also in various skills.

Our productivity in manufacturing, construction, and many services now lags that achieved by others. At the same time, we continue to maintain a high standard of living and consume more than we can afford or even need. This is the American way. We have become the most litigious, self-important, and self-delusional society. Most TV and other broadcasts start with a self-congratulatory statement claiming that it is the world's best coming from the center of the world and is better than all. It does not matter if it is a financial, political or marketing announcement. Somehow we are always told to be aware of our, our products, our technology, our services, and more superiority.

While there are isolated cases where this is still true, there are many where we and everyone else knows that it is or is not true anymore. While the objective may be to raise our morale, there may also be a more sinister one of covering up our and our government/leaders' deficiencies. People who feel good, rightly or wrongly, are assumed to be more easily governable. There is increasing concern that America is vastly over-extended, not just in strategic terms, particularly with the involvement in Iraq and Afghanistan, but its continued military and strategic role in Europe, Japan, and other parts of the world.

Similarly, America continues to lose economic capacity. The growth of the U.S. service industry has greatly reduced the size of the real and potential skilled industrial labor force. This is a major reason for massive outsourcing. U.S. exports are now (December 2010) at an historic low, and agricultural exports, a traditional mainstay of U.S. exports, now only accounts for about 10%. In addition, the low value of the dollar (in international exchange rates) reduces the purchasing power of the export earning.

Interest payable on U.S. foreign debt now exceeds $200b/year or about 1.8% of GDP. Notwithstanding the low value of the dollar, American goods and services have become less competitive. A major reason we have not been able to negotiate attractive and effective trade agreements. While some claim that this is partly due to America's high tax rates, the reality actually indicates otherwise. While income taxes for both individuals and corporations are as high or higher than those in other countries, most other countries impose much higher consumption taxes on gasoline, liquor, cigarettes, and value added taxes on all other manufactured goods. In the U.S., except for federal income, we do have some state and municipal income and sales taxes, but there are usually lower than those imposed by our foreign competitors.

As noted, America is not only the world's most indebted country but also suffers under a declining economy, output capacity, disintegrating infrastructure, and a load of long-term obligations or commitments made when its economic and strategic powers and positions were vastly superior. Now it may require painful changes in culture, habits, expectations, and commitments to work it out of these predicaments.

5.1 Solving America's Problems and Saving Its Future

America, as noted, has in recent years replicated the mistakes of other great powers in history such as the Egyptians, Greeks, Macedonians, Persians, Romans, Chinese, and Ottomans who lost their world power and empires after long success to both external pressure and internal decay. Internal decay had many aspects such as corruption, greed, self-deceit, outright waste, and lack of social responsibility. People were not only becoming increasingly wasteful, particularly in their consumption of everything from clothing and appliances to food and general supplies, but their addictions for excess consumption were fed by government incentives and "expert" recommendations.

A few years ago, for example, the government decided to send everyone a check for $250 to rev up consumption so as to stimulate the economy. I had the audacity of telling the administration that it would have been more efficient to send that money directly to China instead of having American consumers use it to purchase Chinese goods in America.

America's prosperity and leadership was built up over 2-3 hundred years, mainly by immigrants fleeing persecution and poverty from Europe, initially later supported by African and East Asian immigrant workers, most of who came involuntarily. Much of the indigenous Native American population was defeated and often herded into so-called reservations, where they had limited rights.

America's freedoms, huge land mass, and natural resources were well used by these immigrants who developed the world's largest economy, a unique democratic system of government and institutions which became examples for and the envy of most of the world. Throughout the 20th century America ruled supreme as an economic and strategic power where they can work and contribute to society and the economy, instead of costing tax payers billions of dollars and filling up scarce jail cells. In 2010 over 2 million minor offenders were incarcerated.

This is particularly shameful and wasteful when at the same time some major criminals, particularly among financial service executives go free or obtain a pat on the hand. In fact, our legal system is highly discriminatory and is unfairly strict with minor offenders, while major offenders often get away with minor punishments. For example, major offenders such as the CEO and CFO of Countrywide mortgage company which was if not the major instigator in the sub-prime mortgage disaster which not only caused U.S. and later world banking to be undermined, paid a paltry penalty of $67.5 million which bears no relationship either to his money he and his company misappropriated nor the losses they caused. By comparison, the celebrated fashion and style guru Martha Stewart who used insider information to save her a stock loss of about $45,000 went to jail for 5 months plus other punishments.

America has a higher percentage of jail inmates than any other Western country and spends more on incarceration as well as criminal justice or law enforcement as well. This is not mainly because the country is more lawless, but appears to be largely the result of the way the legal system works when minor criminals are subjected to the same rigor and process than major societal and economic criminals.

The system is driven largely by an overzealous legal profession. America has more than twice the number of lawyers in percentage terms than any other Western country or country in general. Furthermore, lawyers in America are much more aggressive than anywhere else. Only in America do lawyers use advertisement and TV announcements as well as other marketing approaches to drum up business. Ambulance chasing is largely an American invention as are large class action suits which are filed on behalf of a large number of supposed injured parties. However, when a settlement is reached, the injured usually end up with a few crumbs, with lawyers pocketing the bulk of the damage payments. America has twice as many lawyers than engineers or doctors. It is important to remember that they not only waste the public's time and money, but also waste a lot of taxpayer funds. In fact, in America more than half of all the money spent on law enforcement contributes nothing to public safety or lawfulness. We could probably improve both public safety and lawfulness by reducing much of this waste in our law enforcement and criminal justice system.

Another wasteful complication is the lack of centralization of criminal justice and law enforcement with one multi-tier system from local police to state police to federal law enforcement, with often overlapping jurisdiction and duties. This largely overlapping and wasteful system has law enforcement,

5.2 Saving America's Agenda

There are a number of strategic actions that could help save America from its self-imposed decline.

1. **Health care** has become the major national drain on the economy and federal as well as state budgets. It is estimated that the total cost of health care will reach nearly $3 trillion by 2012 or about 20.8% of the nation's GDP. Yet less than 50% of that amount will actually be spent on medical procedures, care, medicines, rehabilitation, and related expenses. The rest or nearly $1.5 trillion will be spent on:

- Malpractice insurance
- Other types of insurance
- Marketing of health care and related facilities and services, as well as medicines and other products which have to be prescribed by medical doctors.
- Cost of manual data management and communications
- Labor intensive management
- Inefficient housekeeping
- Disintegrated and disjointed medical and health care services.
- Overlap and duplication of services
- Over-manning of health care facilities with untrained and often incompetent staff
- Sale and use of unproven and sometimes harmful treatments, services or products

2. **Education** is another area where America wastes nearly 50% of expenditures for unnecessary services, over and often incompetent management, wasteful prestige expenditures which add little if anything to education and direct or indirect self-serving or corruption. Out of about $2.8 trillion estimated to be spent on education (public and private); again about 50% will be wasted. About $1.4 trillion will be spent on:

- Over administration, use of unnecessary service, etc. In most school districts, less than 50% of the budget goes for direct educational expenditures, such as teachers, teacher's aids, librarian, etc. salaries, school facilities, etc.

- Inefficient support services such as food, sports, health care, etc.

The rest is spent on direct and indirect administrative costs, public relations, prestige projects, and other expenses.

Few offer high level professional programs. By comparison, European and East as well as South Asian colleges or tertiary educational institutions are mostly focused on professional programs, education, and research. Few among these, for example, encourage people aspiring to work as secretaries, nurses or low-level administrators to attend a 4-year liberal arts or BA program. Instead, most go directly to professional training and in most cases qualify young people in one year or less to work for and perform in such professions unlike the U.S. where secretaries, clerks, nurses, and even many store clerks and others are encouraged to first attend a 4-year college or liberal arts school where they essentially learn what they should have learned in high school. As a result, nearly 82% of high school leavers only join the work force at age 21 or 22 or nearly 4 years or more later than students in those other countries as there are not enough public and not-for-profit universities and colleges to accommodate such a large number of high school leavers.

3. **Law enforcement** is also another area where a significant percentage of expenditures (both public and private) are wasted on frivolous law enforcement (for example, using policemen to divert traffic for minor road work, etc.), public safety or related activities. Total law enforcement expenditure in the U.S. is expected to grow to over $2.4 trillion by 2012, with much of this wasted on frivolous law challenges, inefficient or unnecessary security and public safety activities, corrupt practices, and lack of law enforcement agency integration, coordination or cooperation.

- The largest waste is for mostly frivolous class action suits which do not serve the public but only predatory lawyers. The public or injured parties usually obtain a pittance for damages, with the lawyer racking up a fortune largely at the economy's or public expense.
- Disproportional numbers of blacks and other minorities are incarcerated, many as repeat offenders, a large number for minor or non-violent offenses. Little effort is made to educate minority young and particularly released prisoners. Similarly, few if any employment opportunities exist or are being developed for them. So repeat offenders are frequently

recommitted and former prisoners know little else, have never experienced another life, and are not given effective guidance or training. We should learn from experience abroad. For example, in Israel, universities and trade schools offer for credit or license preparation courses in prison all over the country. This not only trains prisoners for life after prison, but also gives their prison life content. It was found to also improve prisoners' behavior, interpersonal relations as well, as greatly reduce re-incarceration. Prisoners usually pay for the instruction out of money they make from prison work and are after completion or graduation interviewed by prospective employers who may even offer then jobs after completion of their sentences. The program was also found to greatly improve the social environment in prisons, reduce violence, and reduce overall cost of maintaining the prison system.

- Similarly, professional courses taught in prisons for credit cannot only reduce prison violence and boredom but also give incentives and hope to prisoners. It also increases or improves interpersonal relationships and reduces boredom. Prison learning centers are a real improvement in prisoner rehabilitation.

6.0 Rebuilding America

General

America may have to introduce radical changes if it is to regain or retain its economic, strategic, and cultural positions and permit them to grow! In recent years it has lost much of its leadership in some essential areas, most importantly in economic growth. There are many reasons for this and some we hope are reversible, but to halt the decline some drastic and sometimes painful actions may have to be taken.

America is still, though barely, the economic, strategic, and technological leader in the world, though it is being challenged in all these areas and has lost much of its credibility and influence which in turn resulted in loss of faith in its leadership. It has become the world's biggest debtor and is falling behind in science, technology, and even health care and education. Its political systems are being corrupted by narrow interests and lack of focused and committed leadership.

Promises are not kept and the public interests are increasingly ignored in favor of narrow parochial and often financial interests. Washington is no longer the center of the American people's representatives but a huge urban center of lobbyists and representatives with narrow interests, many of which do not benefit the people or America as a nation. In fact, our democratic representative form of government has been greatly corrupted by the infiltration and growing influence of special interests.

Much of this is driven by financial and economic incentives and money instead of the people's interests has become the principal driving force in much of the policy making in Washington. Older democracies such as England have strict limitations on the amount of time and financial support legislators are allowed for their election and after election outside influences and incentives are strictly limited. In America, lobbying and parochial support of the political processes from election to policy making seem to be not only wide open to parochial interests but lawmakers are increasingly influenced by special interests to the exclusion of the general public or the people's interests.

America has become increasingly self laudatory and the self-praising which often ignores real facts and the increasing doubt or even loss of credibility and esteem abroad. This unbridled self-adoration undermines any critical review of reality and is a major factor in the accelerating decline in America's abilities and influence in the wider world. Just saying we are best, greatest or richest does not necessarily make it so and in fact contribute greatly to our lack of realism in our political, economic, social, and strategic dealings in the world.

Rebuilding America will require determined efforts in restructuring our political, educational, health care, financial services, and socio-economic systems as discussed and make changes in our ways and self-perception. There are a number of major areas which must be rebuilt without delay if we are to save America.

6.1 Rebuilding America's Education

America had a most superb education system developed over its history which triggered the establishment of some of the world's greatest universities and particularly the concept of research universities. Many of the greatest universities or centers of research, science, and learning were established by private citizens, while states developed parallel public universities.

In more recent years, a large number of liberal arts colleges and later for-profit private universities were established and now dominate the field or tertiary or college education in America. This is very different from developments in other advanced countries where the central government takes a direct role in education from primary and secondary to tertiary or college education. This not only assures nationwide level and quality control, but also assures a fair and equal level of financial support which is now lacking in the U.S. where poor districts are usually penalized by lower per student budgets when they actually need bigger budgets to make up for the lack of home and community support and facilities.

This seems to be a major reason for the continued lower achievements of poor (often minority) neighborhood children in school. This is contrary to approaches in other, particularly developed countries, where generally schools are under the control of and financed by the central government. This way, uniform levels and content of education can and are being achieved.

Many feel that the American approach of using local taxes to finance primary and secondary education perpetuates discrimination and is a major factor in the lack of performance of poor and often minority or immigrant children. In other words, the system is a major cause for the continued poverty and lack of upward mobility of poor often minority or immigrant children.

In general, teacher's salaries are low and so is their social status and respect. As most have tenure and are also otherwise protected by union rules, changes in the American public school systems are hard to make and take a long time. With local control, politics often plays a major role not only in budget decisions but also in the approach to contents or quality of subjects being taught. Similarly, school budgets are often highly distorted by prestige priorities such as expenditures for competitive prestige sports such as American football and basketball which require massive budgets, yet involve usually just a very small number of students, while other, less prestigious sports such as athletics, fútbol (soccer), etc. get very little support.

In some parts of the country, attempts are made to correct some of the discrimination towards poor district and particularly minority children by busing them to better schools in more affluent neighborhoods. This though has the disadvantage of moving children into a completely different, and in a way strange, neighborhood or environment where they are surrounded by children of more affluent households with different experiences, aspirations, and cultural interests. With prevailing competitive spirits among children, bused kids may feel even more estranged and even discriminated as they cannot fairly compete in studies or social activities with their peers.

In most other countries, primary and secondary schools are funded by the central governments with poor neighborhood schools actually rewarded with budget extras to not only allow them to offer comparable programs but also extracurricular facilities and activities to help students who have little or insufficient facilities or support at home for their homework or remedial studies/activities.

In recent years, the quality and general performance of primary and secondary education in the U.S. has declined precipitously. While a few decades ago, American students were among top achievers in math and sciences, their performance has fallen appreciably in recent years and is now at the level of many developing countries. The situation seems to be equally bad at the secondary or high school level as in primary education and even the introduction of so-called charter schools has had little effect in improving overall quality. Various federal programs such as "No Child Left Behind" and others seem to be nice slogans but have little effect on the quality of education. It seems that much more fundamental changes may be needed and possibly a revamping of the entire way education is organized, financed, and administered may be required. It may be time to learn from the experience of other Western Democratic Free Market economy countries such as Western Europe and even Japan.

In all of these, primary and secondary education is largely administered and financed by the central and not the local government which usually funds schooling equitably, sets national standards and priorities, and assures the effective training, retraining, and certification of teachers who are given professional level salaries and benefits, proper prestige and status, and meaningful recognition and continuous training and retraining. With nationwide uniform standards and support, teachers are given the job security needed and wanted.

6.1.1 Primary and Secondary Education

As noted, unlike in most developed and developing countries, primary and secondary education in America is usually financed and controlled locally. This has both advantages and disadvantages. On one hand, it permits programs and facilities to be custom designed for local requirements, yet at the same time it often results in large differences in funding of education and as a result quality of instruction, facilities, and support which more often than not discriminates against children in poor neighborhoods.

In fact, many children in poor neighborhoods neither have quiet and comfortable rooms or facilities to do their homework nor adults to help them with it if they require assistance or support. This means that such children actually need more after school support, both in terms of facilities and guidance. However, the opposite is usually true which makes it that much harder to help poor and disadvantaged children to emerge from poverty and often also discrimination through education which is supposed to be the ultimate equalizer.

It serves as such in many other countries and could achieve greater and easier integration and advance from poverty, but it may require more than busing which simply gives some poor neighborhood children an opportunity to learn with those of richer neighborhoods, but it only makes them even more aware of the basic differences in standards of living, expectation, and support.

A better solution and the approach used in most other developed countries is that education is funded by the central government with equal budgets for all students and additional funds for special services and facilities.

Table 4: Incentives for Improving Education
In most places with superior education systems, certain measures seem to dominate such as:
1. Assure that teachers work both with salaries and conditions commensurate with that of respected professionals such as lawyers, doctors or engineers.
2. Celebrate academic achievements at least as much as achievements in sport.
3. Encourage at least as much competitive spirit and incentives in academic subjects as in sports, theatrics, and other entertaining activities.
4. Install proper reward systems for students, teachers, and schools.

America has the largest percentage of college attendees among any country in the world. More than 84% of high school leavers go on to college versus about half as many in most European countries, Japan, and Korea. In China, a bare 16% of high school leavers go on to college. The vast majority of American high school graduates go on to liberal arts colleges which often offer a curriculum very similar to that of a good high school. In fact, most of these teach essentially high school programs and could be called remedial high schools.

6.1.2 College Education

As noted, most high school leavers attend liberal arts colleges or programs where they do not obtain any marketable skills nor do they usually develop effective job or career plans. As a result, they basically spend another 3-4 years in school without advancing their job or career skills. This issue has become even more acute in recent years with the large-scale emergence of for-profit colleges which are much less discriminatory or demanding in their admissions standards. They similarly are quite aggressive in their marketing and help potential applicants in their student loan applications.

Recent studies show that over 85% of their graduates do not find employment in the area in which they supposedly qualified. As a result, most of these graduates default on their student loans which cost the taxpayer billions of dollars per year. However, there are much larger costs to the U.S. economy, resulting from this avalanche of college attendees. As a result of this trend, 84% of high school leavers or about 3 million young people per year lose 10% or 4 years of their working life, career building, and earning potential. In addition, they are often imputed with false or unrealistic hopes and expectations.

6.1.3 Economic Impact of the Skewed American Education System

In addition to the loss of earnings and output resulting from the loss of 10% of the working life of 84% of young Americans, there is a loss of about 8% of contributions to Social Security, health care, and other social support program contributions, as these young people are covered by all these social and health care support programs but only start contributing to them about 3-4 years later than those in other countries.

Then there is also a loss in working skills. As most high school leavers opt for college, whether appropriate or not, there is now and has been for years a dearth of graduates of trade schools, community colleges, and other training programs designed to train people for new manufacturing, design, construction, and similar careers. In fact, increasingly a reason for outsourcing or emigration of manufacturing jobs, etc. is no longer low labor cost but lack of availability of skilled or trained, motivated workers in the U.S.

This problem is getting worse all the time, as America continues to encourage the growth of service industries and activities. Smaller countries such as Singapore, a resource poor island nation of 5 million, started as an all-service economy, but its leaders soon recognized that this does not work in the long run and rapidly encouraged and induced the development of specialized manufacturing which served the country well and assured a balanced near full employment economy ever since.

It is essential that the American economy similarly be balanced and support thriving manufacturing, construction, agricultural, and technology development sectors and reduces its economic dependence on services and particularly consumption. However, educational programs are not focused on this. The percentage of college graduates in science and engineering is declining all the time and is now less than half of these in other developed countries. At the same time, we graduate several times as many people in law, insurance, and other services as any other country in the world. We do not train or encourage education in fields where there are ready made jobs, but in services we never knew we needed.

America has some of the world's most renowned colleges and universities, centers of learning which are at the forefront of research and knowledge globally. While many state universities in America are excellent and offer great education, the most illustrious centers of learning in America are private universities such as the Ivy League (Harvard, Yale, Princeton, MIT, etc.), In fact, while the concept of research universities was not originally developed in the U.S., it was extended and brought to fruition here. In fact, it was in the U.S. where the close relationships between universities, government, and industry was first developed and expanded. The bulk of the budget of the research universities now comes from funded research and not from tuition.

The big research universities have all been very successful not only in their programs and research results, but also in their contributions to the U.S. and world economies. For example, MIT graduates founded hundreds of successful companies, often based on the research they performed at MIT. For many years, these universities attracted large numbers of foreign students who usually joined or formed American companies after graduation.

In more recent years, a growing number of successful graduates returned to their home countries, such as China, India, Korea, Taiwan, and Japan to form or join companies there often based on research and knowledge they acquired while working at a U.S. university. We should make it more attractive for such foreign nations to start or join an enterprise here to assure better control of the use and exploitation of such research results or technological advances.

Another important issue is continued education. Technology and its uses are advancing so rapidly now that it is essential to provide and support continuous education at the craft or trade as well as post-graduate levels. The speed of technological and knowledge advances is so great now that it is essential to continuously retrain people at all levels. Here again America lags many other countries in continuous education or training. Such retraining must become routine and government must provide both oversight as well as incentives for retraining such as tax deductions and special awards and recognition. In fact, it may be necessary to require proof of retraining to be able to renew a license. This will be necessary to maintain competitive technology and productivity levels in all professions from shop floor to research, design, and technology developments.

There must also be a major improvement in incentives provided to engineering, technology, manufacturing, construction, and other professions essential for the economic and technological revival, advance, and competitive posture of the U.S. yet which lagged service sector jobs in their rewards, advances, and opportunities in both economic rewards as well as status.

It is increasingly important to maintain the American human capital base and assure retraining, reeducation, and technological/skill advance of people in all professions and all skill and/or responsibility levels. We must develop more coordinated and higher quality programs that assure maintenance of the highest, most advanced skill and knowledge levels, for all jobs and all professionals. Similarly, we urgently require better and enforceable quality requirements in all educational programs, with both incentives and penalties for teachers, professors, and trainers in all areas and at all levels.

Teaching and instructing must not be a job or career of last resort, but a prestigious career with appropriate rewards, respect, and advancement opportunities. The economic impact of the American education system is huge. Consider the loss of at least 50% of high school leavers who should be in the job market one year or less after graduating from high school and learning a trade in 6-12 months. Such a development would increase the U.S. workforce by about 8.2% total, with a larger increase in manufacturing, construction, and technology development and only a small gradual decline in the number of people in service jobs. In total, rough estimates show that such a strategy could increase America's GDP by about 6.9%, exports by 4.2%, and contribution to Social Security by about 6.2%.

Such developments would go a long way in making Social Security and other social support programs financially viable, decrease our foreign trade imbalance or deficit, and move us closer to balancing our budget. In the longer run, it would also give us excess revenues to repay some of our foreign debts.

6.2 Rebuilding America's Law Enforcement System

America spends more on law enforcement and related activities than any other nation or about 13.8% of GDP. Much of this is for low level or frivolous crime fighting such as incarceration of minor drug and similar offenders. About 1-2 million people in U.S. prisons or about 60% are minor, non-violent criminals who could be punished by committing them to supervised, restricted work programs which serve to both keep these people supervised and under control, yet mentally and economically active so as to both maintain the active participants in society and involved in self-improvement and skill development.

In parallel, there is an urgent need to follow the example of other countries such as Israel where formal for-credit or license courses or programs are given to non-violent prisoners. This not only assures that they learn and qualify for jobs in certain skills of their choosing and therefore prepare them for a productive job and life outside prison, but it also assures an interesting and satisfying life in prison. This, it was found, contributed to more harmonious life and interrelationships in prison, easier maintenance of order, and more cooperative inmates.

As prisoners would usually pay for the instruction from work earnings, the costs of such a program are actually negative. The percentage of repeat offenders is shown to decline rapidly and permanently. Overall, this approach can easily save 8-15% of the cost of incarceration, but more importantly add 3-6% to the productive workforce at no cost to society. Among other savings from changes in the law enforcement system is radical tort reform. Here two issues dominate.

1. Legal and health care cost savings from radical tort reform. Malpractice insurance and related costs amount to over 30% of total health care costs, but they also add major costs to law enforcement costs (court, investigative, insurance, etc.). Most importantly, they force the use of defensive medical procedures which add significantly to the costs and performance of health care.

Replacing malpractice and related procedures by compulsory professional arbitration before courts of experts could reduce both the law enforcement and health care costs significantly. In fact, as medical experts are anyway called in to any court or legal procedure, why not leave out the lawyers and court room and perform the whole procedure before a group of medical experts who form an arbitration council with full powers to revoke the license and/or impose monetary damages to be paid for by the doctor, hospital or clinic. In many countries, such professional councils or boards issue licenses and have the legal powers to revoke licenses as well as impose monetary damages or awards.

The approach has the power of a legal or court procedure without the huge legal and court costs and waste of time involved. Furthermore, the subject under review is restricted to the medical issues. Such approaches are used successfully in construction, as medical claim procedures successfully, at a fraction of the cost and time legal malpractice and similar issues are dealt with in courts.

There are other areas in law enforcement where huge economic savings can be obtained. For example, "class actions" brought by a lawyer against a manufacturer, service provider or operator is an action whereby a lawyer or law firm identified a large number of people or parties involved in or affected by some fault in a service or product. By assembling a large number of assumed affected people and/or parties, huge claims for the combined damage caused can be made.

Lawyers who identify and organize class actions will usually assume the identification and analysis of the issue and then combine the claims of all those affected or damaged into one case. As individual claims would be too small to justify legal representation, combining these claims permits the class action to demand large enough damages to justify and make it attractive to high power lawyers or law firms who usually work on a contingency basis with 25% or more of damages assigned retained as fees by the lawyers, and the remainder divided among the claimants.

These procedures are very inefficient, take huge amounts of time from claimants, lawyers, and defendants. Though fair, it is an extremely inefficient system and seldom results in satisfactory results. Claimants may have to waste hundreds of hours to finally get a pittance of a few dollars as a reward or less recuperation. The lawyers never lose but thousands of hours are wasted for largely frivolous efforts.

6.3 ECONOMICS OF FAIR TAXATION

Although many Americans complain about high taxation, in fact they are among the least taxed citizens in modern developed countries. In America, we primarily pay federal and state (and sometimes also municipal) income taxes, gasoline, cigarettes, and liquor consumption, and some sales taxes; all these, in addition to sizeable local real estate taxes. Others though while their corporate and/or individual income tax may be lower usually pay much higher consumption taxes. For example, gasoline and other fuel or energy taxes in Europe, East Asia, and more are usually 3-4 times as high as those in the U.S.

In addition, most other Western countries and others impose a Value Added Tax or VAT which in many countries is as high as 15% or more on everything bought or bartered. If we add all these taxes, we find that while income taxes in many cases are lower than those in the U.S., the total tax burden is usually significantly higher. This brings up the point of fairness of income versus consumption taxes, with the latter assumed to be a greater burden for lower income earners, while the earlier affects higher income earners more.

Use of low consumption taxes encourages wasteful consumption in America. In fact, some studies indicate that if the U.S. would tax gasoline, etc. at the European rate U.S. oil import requirements would decline by at least 30%, with a parallel improvement in air quality. While we consider taxes on tobacco, liquor, etc. sin taxes which are good for us, no similar argument is usually advanced concerning gasoline or fuel taxes. Similarly, changing our tax system by scaling it more towards the rich has not been popular notwithstanding the fact that a maximum tax rate of 38% or barely more than twice the minimum tax rate of 15% seems a little odd.

In fact, U.S. income taxes in the past and taxes in several Western countries go very much higher and do not level off at 38% on incomes of middle class earners as in the U.S. where wealthy pay only the middle class income tax rate for all income above a normal middle class income. This seems not only unfair but also highly inefficient as it rewards but earners unfairly on account of workers and middle class earners who in America pay an inordinately large percentage of total taxes though their combined earnings are much smaller than those of the top 2% or 4% earners.

6.4 Balancing the Budget and Paying Off the National Debt

Simple calculations show that if we had the political will and support to introduce the suggested changes in education/employment, law enforcement and legal procedures, and taxation, we could not only balance our budget without serious or any cuts in social entitlements, defense, and government, and still have enough left over to service as well as gradually pay off our foreign and domestic debt, as well as rebuild our infrastructure and convert America into a truly modern, well equipped, and managed society. Obviously, this would require not only a lot of political will power as well as a willingness to put the interest of the country and its people and future generations of Americans up front and ahead of those of narrow, short term interests of various vocal yet influential minority interests with political clout and/or large lobbying budgets.

America will have to make a choice if it wants to remain a great nation and leader with a social conscience and democratic agenda under which it not only satisfies immediate and narrow interests, but truly takes care of maintaining and growing America as a beacon of Western civilization, a free market democracy in which all citizens enjoy a decent life, opportunities and freedoms, and have a government that truly is by the people and for the people.

Over the last decade or since the start of the 21st century, America has lost not only much of its economic importance and clout, but also much of its leadership in many areas of technology, manufacturing, logistics, and more. It will have to make major investments to regain the leadership position it held just a few years ago. It is not too late to recapture the past, but act we must, including the introduction of some painful decisions, such as lowering of our greedy consumption, our willingness to pay taxes so that we can provide better health care, education, infrastructure, and safety. We have been too greedy and self-centered or selfish for too long; all this on account of other or our own future generations. We must focus more on what we need and how to get it effectively and not just what we want.

Asia is emerging rapidly as a challenger in economic, technological, and strategic terms, and in many areas is already a leader. Their approach is very different and China in particular is governed centrally by a group of technocrats who set strategies, priorities, budgets, and allocation. It is not a free market democracy which gives it certain advantages which are particularly important now when technology changes so rapidly and affects everything so much.

Our free market democratic economy has much more momentum and is much harder to subject to rapid and large changes which today's technological inertia demands. However, we have the advantage of free-wheeling scientists and engineers who are envisioning and inventing new technology all the time. The plan offered here is true to all American principles and designed to put the country back on its feet, economically, financially, logistically, technologically, culturally, and most importantly into a true, long-term world leadership position.

It is designed to assure that America does not follow predecessor global leaders throughout history like China, Persia, Egypt, Rome, Ottomans, the USSR, and others whose empires fell apart soon after they reached the pinnacle of their power, influence, and prosperity. In most cases, greed, lack of regulation and lawlessness, loss of focus and civilization as well as respect for others undermined their position and led to their loss of leadership, power, and ultimately wealth and well being.

Rebuilding America will require reorganization and retraining of our human capital by developing a better balance of trained people. We must return to a system where people are trained for jobs available or needed and not just to satisfy some dreams or sales concept. In a way, do what our forefathers did in directing and preparing their children for jobs, careers, and opportunities, and not just let them walk off into a dream world or follow some pied piper. The latter has not become the norm and not just the exception, and fewer and fewer young people commit and prepare themselves for jobs that are bound to be available and that interest them and make use of their talents, abilities, and interests.

At the moment, we provide many unrealistic goals and induce many of our young to attend college with neither a goal or even focused interest nor an understanding of what college education is for or what they expect to achieve or gain from a college education which will cost them or the taxpayer a lot of money and the student 3-4 years of their lives. This is not only a personal waste but also a public waste because as much as 10% of our potential work output is squandered. This not only makes America poorer, but also affects the world at large as we consume public goods independent of the total life work input we provide. If we on average work 10% fewer years then we produce 10% less, yet consume the same in materials and services.

America's economy has become more and more dependent on input from abroad and we have less and less to offer to pay for what we import and consume. Even in services, a growing percentage are now imported and information and communication technologies and services now permit even sales, advisory, and other information services to be imported. This is a very dangerous situation not only because it drives up our trade imbalance and as a result foreign debt, but it also reduces employment in the U.S. and transfers not just technology but also trade, manufacturing, and marketing technologies and approaches. Many of our technical, trade, service, and marketing secrets are being exported and then used to compete with us, our trading, our products, and services.

6.5 American Wealth

America grew and prospered for centuries on Puritan values, a rich country, and a very liberal and fair government. It grew from a country of poor immigrants who largely lived off the land to a great modern, largely industrial, society. Traditional approaches and values, particularly Puritanism, lost importance and were replaced by selfishness, greed, and often dishonesty. Washington, once a center of lively discussion and public discourse, has become a center of lobbyists, narrow interests, and money.

Public discussion has been largely replaced by influence peddling. Though elections are still fair, few politicians, once elected, remember or support issues, programs, and developments they promised their constituents or do they truly represent them. Lofty promises of accessibility and true representation are hardly ever followed. Mail boxes are always full and calls are never returned. True, some occasionally sneak in a little project which benefits the home base, but in general the people Representatives and Senators are beholding to narrow, big interests.

The cost of running for office has now quadrupled in just 20 years and even the more invasive publicity technology of today demands huge expenditures which are now largely financed by narrow, not necessarily the people's, interests. We bailed out the major banks with taxpayer money, yet as soon as they were out of the woods, they immediately restarted paying outrageous salaries and bonuses.

In parallel, the wealthy mounted a huge campaign against increases in taxation or at least continuation of the tax cuts. Today the wealth of the top 5% of Americans is estimated to be over $48 trillion or nearly 10 times what it was just 20 years ago. During the same time, wealth of middle class which make up 25% of the population or 5 times the number of wealthy has grown only marginally and barely tripled during that period. However, the poor and middle class pay nearly 95% of all the taxes. As noted, Americans have among the lowest tax burdens of any people in developed countries. We urgently need a fairer and more effective tax system, one that rewards success, yet punishes greed, theft, and cheating.

America's wealth and income distribution is extremely skewed and getting more so. In other words, the rich are getting richer and everyone else is getting poorer. At the same time, the economy is skewed towards consumption, but with very little of what we consume made or grown in this country, our foreign debt continues to grow and so will ownership of domestic assets by foreigners until much of our assets will be owned by foreigners. Then we will obviously lose control and many of the benefits of ownership of productive assets. This in parallel with the skewed wealth and income distribution among Americans may challenge the American dream, in terms of income, living standards, way of life, and our socio/political system. America grew and developed a prosperous and productive society largely on the basis of its maintenance of Puritan values.

Ignoring or discarding these values and contents in our way of life is doing irreparable damage to America and all we stand for and value. A society in which the top 2-5% of citizens grew wealth 5 times as fast and earns 20 times as much as an average, productive middle class citizen is not sustainable. It is and will increasingly lose not only its physical assets and property, but also its productive capacity. This invariably must lead to a complete decline and ultimate loss of relevance in the world economy.

America has lost much of its economic prowess built up during and after two devastating world wars. It is now losing much of its entrepreneurship and global competitiveness, yet most importantly it is losing the faith and trust of its own people and the world at large.

6.6 Savings Formula

It is increasingly evident that America must change if it wants to retain or regain its economic, social, financial, and cultural leadership of the world, the faith of its own people, and others around the world. However, this is only possible if it and its people are willing and able to make hard and unpopular decisions and change our ways. This will include radical changes in our education, health care, law enforcement, political system, and financial institutions. We must return to some of the values of Puritanism and our forefathers. We must return decency, honesty, and courtesy to our political institutions and assure that they act on behalf of the people who elected them and keep their promises.

In fact, election and appointments must become a legal contract which becomes null and void if a representative does not act in line with promises and undertakings on the basis of which he/she were elected. The time has come to get honesty back into politics and government. Similarly, governing requires professionalism, management skills, honesty, and commitment. We need more trained professionals or technocrats in government, not just party hacks.

We must return to purer, free market democratic principles under which bribing, including political bribing and lobbying, is outlawed. We must make sure that our representatives truly represent the people who elected them, not the highest bidder. Finally, and most importantly, we must increase our productivity and output, and reduce our consumption. We must get and buy what we need, not what we want or are told to acquire and make sure we use and consume it. We must introduce and practice continuous learning and relearning.

Most importantly, we must learn to judge ourselves and be self-critical. For too long we have sunk under exaggerated self-perception, self-praise, and indulgence. It is time we learn to judge ourselves and fairly evaluate our real accomplishments, abilities, and performances. While we are good at many things, we are not the best at or in everything. So let us get to work and clean up our house, get our economy in order, and get ready for a renewed and glorious American future.

7.0 Conclusions

American global leadership in essence is over and its unique dominion actually lasted only two to three decades as noted by Haas.[23] After World War II, it was shared with Russia for over three decades. Today America is not only challenged as a political and strategic but also economic and technological leader. It has become weaker in relations to old foes, but also traditional allies such as Western European nations by encouraging their unification at least in economic terms. It has also become much more dependent on global supplies. U.S. energy demand has grown precipitously and it now imports twice as much as a percentage of national consumption than it did in 1970. The results were increasing trade deficits and transfer of wealth to other mainly oil exporting countries and China. In addition, the costly wars in Iraq and Afghanistan and the sub-prime mortgage disaster added to the huge fiscal account deficits and national debt, largely to foreign creditors.

These trends were accelerated by globalization which facilitated cross border transactions. The question, as yet unanswered, is will American dominance be replaced by a single or multi-polar world in which several powerful nations as a group or groups replace American domination. Such a world may be much more complex as unity of purpose and direction of development may become increasingly elusive.

7.1 The Issue of World Over-population and Our Demographic Riddle

We are facing a threat of over-population in this first century of the third millennium.[24] Although many have opinioned that Thomas Malthus' dire predictions 170 years ago were a fallacy, today's realities force us to reconsider. At the same time, humanity nearly sextupled in the last two centuries; yet standards of living and the quality of life in general improved significantly during that period. People today are healthier

23   Haas, Richard, "What follows American Dominion", *Financial Times*, April 16, 2008.
24   Jacoby, Jeff, "The Coming Population Bust", *International Herald Tribune*, June 24, 2008.

and live significantly longer lives which also contributed greatly to the world's population.

The world population is still rising even though average birth rates are generally below the replacement level, with the exception of America, some parts of South America, Africa, most Moslem countries, and India. But the increase is marginal and may not be sustained. Some countries such as Russia are losing 700,000 people per year and many European countries barely maintain their population level, and this only through massive immigration, largely by Moslems who themselves maintain high birth rates. As a result, the population of most European countries is expected to present a very different demographic composition by the middle of the century. In Europe the number of children under 5 has declined by 38% from 1960 to 2008.

Fertility rates are dropping seriously, particularly in non-Moslem countries where women work, have more freedoms, and usually marry later or not at all. The results are not only fewer babies or a non-replacement birth rate, but a diminishing working age population only temporarily slowed by increases in the number of working women. At the same time, the ratio of retired to working people will continue to escalate largely due to greater longevity, increasing the strain on retirement and health care funding which before long may constitute nearly all public tax-financed expenditures. This reality is approaching faster than ever imagined and may require radical increase in the retirement age, child support, and various other measures, so well presented by Phillip Longman in an interview in the documentary "Demographic Winter: The Decline of the Human Family".

7.2 America's Future

America has become the most wasteful society on earth and confirms its irrational consumption and waste spree, largely because of the rest of the world and its people's consumption and waste driven by greed and insolent demand now without bounds. This trend must be reversed lest we are forced to transfer or sell many of our real assets such as real estate, infrastructure, land, and natural resources to cover and service our foreign debt. Reversing this trend requires radical changes not just in our economy but also our social contracts and the role of government.

In other words, the world of the future may look very different from our present and past. America, in particular, will be affected by these changes as it is more dependent on the world-at-large than most other nations, as a nation of immigrants increasingly dependent on trade and a growing service sector with declining production. America is facing a dire future unless it is able to make radical changes in its economy, social contracts, and role in the world. This may have to include a realization that the role of America has and will continue to change and that as part of it, America may have to adjust its social contracts, way of life, and role in the world.

America is no longer the greatest, most productive, richest, most affluent, and most advanced nation in the world. It has many admirable characteristics and an interesting lifestyle, but the time has come to consider changes in many things we consider American and in some a birthright as an American. As noted before, we may have to introduce incentives for people to learn a trade or skill right after high school and/or train for a job or work for which there is a definite demand. We cannot have a nation where most people have college degrees but no skills or professional credentials.

We cannot have a nation where an increasing number of citizens are incarcerated for minor crimes at public expense without reducing the potential of a repeat of their infraction. We must retrain and redirect much of our prison population. The majority of our prisoners are now repeat offenders and this percentage is growing.

We urgently need a way to improve education and job training. Many of the prisoners come from low income environments, with low educational achievements. In other words, a restructuring of our educational system should have a great impact on crime and our law enforcement and incarceration costs. We have to look at these various issues in overall national terms. In other words, better universal education and job training for real and not imaginary jobs will affect our law enforcement requirements and costs. Therefore we cannot just look at centrally financed and controlled universal education as a social and economic issue, it affects everything.

Better universal and job focused education affects health, the economy, and law enforcement. In fact, studies indicate that additional expenses for universal (uniform) education and focused job training will save twice as much in law enforcement and health care. In addition to the large savings possible in education by reducing the number of unnecessary college admissions and training people for real jobs savings in health care and savings in law enforcement which together (Table

7.1) are estimated to account for over $1.2 trillion per year, enough to cover our budget deficit and permit continuation of most of our entitlement programs, there are many potential savings in reducing waste (both service as well as consumption waste) and unnecessary wasted investments.

America generates about 2-3 times as much solid, liquid, and air pollution waste per capita than any other country and is responsible for nearly half the world's air, solid waste and similar pollution. In addition, the costs of waste disposal have skyrocketed in recent years, a process expected to continue indefinitely.

Recycling in the U.S. is quite inefficient and infrastructure maintenance nearly non-existent. We are running out of waste disposal sites. It is essential that we improve our recycling and start to chose or use more readily recyclable material. America's future looks bleak indeed unless we introduce radical changes. It is becoming a country of the rich with a declining middle class, a decrepit lower class, and a dismal future unless radical changes are introduced, adopted, accepted, and actually made. We were all promised "change" by the Obama Administration but it did not occur nor is it effectively planned and supported.

American society is degenerating into a small, greedy, and largely selfish wealth class, a miniscule and declining hard working middle class, and a large and largely dispirited poor class which used to be employed by and aspire to join the middle class. Money and greed have become the principal characteristics of America and American society. While there are still a few with a social conscience and will contribute to the common good, there are few among our leaders and representatives or government who work with the public interest and America's future mainly in mind.

This country was built by its middle class and largely defended by soldiers of the poorer class, yet the benefits and fruits of their efforts and lives are largely reaped by the rich, including increasingly our so-called representatives who instead of representing the people who elected them, increasingly represent special interests and money. While this used to be largely among Republicans and so-called right wing politicians, the trend has infected Democrats as well. In fact, our society is rapidly degenerating into a two class (rich and poor) society in which money means and controls everything and greed is accepted as social grace and a social norm. While this has long developed in the financial business community, it has now also taken over Washington and much of our political processes.

There is an urgent need to curtail the influence and role of lobbyists and other special interests and assure better access to lawmakers and government officials by ordinary, yet concerned citizens. There are many examples of Western democracies where such an approach works and unbiased law making rules prevail. I wish we could return to these good old days when we stood up to injustice and our lawmakers truly represented the people of America and their interests. Today even the U.S. Supreme Court appears to be biased towards special interest when it ruled that corporations, just like citizens, can support politicians and political parties/interests.

Obviously ordinary citizens could never compete with corporations, unions, and other powerful groups or interests in support of politicians. In other words, instead of power to the people and representatives of the people, we should be honest and call our lawmakers and government institutions the representatives of special interests. This is the surest way to the ruin of this country in competition with major, new powerful economies such as China, India, Brazil, and the EU which are governed by more representative lawmakers.

A communist regime such as in China is largely governed by competent technocrats and not political hacks whose loyalty in many cases lies not with the electorate but their financial supporters represented by lobbyists and other influence peddlers. We may not be the most corrupt nation in pure financial terms, but when it comes to politics we probably rule the world. The most important sign of a modern democratic, honest, free market society is in addition to its lawmaking bodies its law enforcement or legal system. Here again our system is highly skewed towards special interests and money. Poor and minor criminals are usually punished severely while large, powerful criminals get off with a slap on the hand.

As an example, Angelo Mozillo of the mortgage company Countrywide who made hundreds of millions, if not billions from fraudulent transactions agreed to pay a fine of $67.5 million but was spared conviction and possible jail time. This is just one example of how our system of law enforcement is always hard on minor crimes or criminals but somehow finds ways to allow major criminals to get away with a pat on the hand. The same seems to apply to other types of crimes. For example, our jails are full of petty drug addicts or users but very few large drug dealers. In fact, there are many who argue that we could save the public billions of dollars by releasing minor offenders, particularly drug offenders to supervised freedom and retraining so that they can truly rejoin society and live productive lives.

The well-to-do and influential cannot only afford to hire the most well connected lawyers but also arrange for more lenient treatment. In America, contrary to the basic tenets of the Constitution, not all are equal under the law. In other words, the law treats you differently depending on your status, wealth, and even location at which the issue is adjudicated.

We must build America's future on more solid foundations, foundations it once had and which served it to emerge as the world's preeminent free market democratic economy and the leader of the world. We unfortunately lost our way in recent years and are now a disjointed people with a highly damaged economy, a dysfunctional government, a non-representative legislature, a people who are primarily consumers with an interest in having their wants satisfied, with little concern with and interest in their contribution to the common good. It has become truly a society of consumers with little concern for their contributions to the general output. Its primary concern is that its wants are met no matter who pays or provides it.

Less than 40 years ago we were the most affluent, productive, and possibly honest, concerned society. So how did this happen and what needs to be done to reverse the situation? The main reasons for the change were:

1. We allowed the three principal institutions of any society, education, health care, and law enforcement to atrophy. All three not only consumed an increasing percentage of our output or GDP, but started to become increasingly inefficient, self-serving, unfocused, and wasteful. As noted, in my 1998 book on "American Institutional Dilemma" (Vantage Press, NY, 1998), no society or nation can allow the cost of these essential institutions to grow by a multiple of its economic growth; yet we did and it became evident then that unless we reigned in the costs of these institutions they would before long compromise our whole economy. In other words, we would produce nothing but education, health care, and law enforcement, yet, at the same time, we let these institutions decline in quality and focus.

7.3 Final Note

To rebuild America it will be necessary to restructure our major institutions such as education, health care, and law enforcement, and make them as well as our social services and laws more responsible to the changed needs of a modern, technologically, advanced society. Most importantly, America must become a less indulgent and more productive society where needs take precedence over wants. This applies to our physical, social, economic, as well as political areas.

7.4 Rebuilding America

As noted, America, like other good empires in history, must bite the bullet and make difficult, hurtful decisions if it and its people want to remain leaders and maintain not only a largely unearned, high standard of living, but also world leadership. Rome, like other major world powers, fell apart and lost the leadership when it degenerated into a largely corrupt self-serving dictatorship, stopped maintaining its infrastructure, and lost contact with its people and their needs. It repeated the experiences of other doomed great empires such as Egypt, China, Persia, Macedonia, and more.

Each of these empires failed when it consumed more than it produced, when special interests took precedence over the interests of the people and the state, when corruption was tolerated, and laws or regulations failed to be enforced or enforced only selectively. When the great concepts of statesmanship, leadership, technology, and organization gave way to narrow personal or other special interests and when the major institutions in education, health care, infrastructure, and supply of essentials were allowed to rot. Rome, for example, was great in advancing access to clean water, safe roads, and other infrastructure which supported commerce and life once these systems fell apart in parallel with increased lawlessness, corruption, and self-serving, the structure of the empire disintegrated. We now witness a repeat of history in our modern 21st century setting, where America, the undisputed richest, most powerful nation in the second half of the 20th century finds itself at a crossroads.

In recent years and in fact since the beginning of the 21st century, America seems to have lost its way in economic, strategic, and socio-cultural terms. It degenerated into a country with an increasing deficit, a faltering economy, faltering institutions such as health care, education, and law enforcement; yet it continued to increase its consumption and to spend way above its means. Politicians, once the representatives of the people, became increasingly beholden to special interests and lost touch with the needs of the people and the nation. At the same time, they continued to involve the country in unnecessary, non-winnable wars and ventures while continuing the piper's marching song.

7.5 Plan for America's Revival

For America to regain its leadership, power, and global respect, it will have to introduce radical changes in its economy, strategic posture, lifestyle, institutions, and ultimately way of life as well as expectations. The major changes required are in education, health care, law enforcement, basic lifestyle, and consumption, strategic (military/power) policy, and infrastructure and public services. All of these changes are designed not so much to remake America but to bring it back to a position of leadership or at least get it back to best practices and quality available. We used to be the leaders not just in technology but also in services, but as noted before have fallen woefully behind in recent years, even in areas where the original technology, service or strategy originated in America.

This, as noted, is true in education, communication, health care, distributed systems (electricity, water, wired telephone, and more), as well as in military operations. Many of the suggestions or plan details may be politically difficult or socially unpopular, but we are now in a situation where as a nation we must be able and willing to make hard decisions in order to not just survive but regain and maintain many of our advantages, needs, and positions.

1. Education. Education is universal in America, but it must become more focused to the needs of the country and its developments. Apart from compulsory primary and secondary education which will have to become more serious and focused. Though there are exceptions, American primary and secondary education lacks in quality far behind that in countries in Europe, China, and even India among other particularly in math and sciences. Furthermore, there are as mentioned huge differences in the quality of education throughout the country. This not only disadvantages students from poor or rural neighborhoods but also contributes to the fact that an inordinate percentage of high school leavers go on to college.

Appendix A: How the Financial Crisis Was Engineered

Financial service institutions, and particularly mortgage brokers and banks, developed a hierarchy of financial instruments whose purpose was to make the huge global mortgage market less transparent and more profitable by arranging financial incentives which permitted the unregulated marketing of opaque mortgage related instruments and funds to an avalanche of traders and aggressive investors. These were far removed from the traditional direct mortgage sale to property owners, with the issuer serving the mortgage directly. Instead, mortgages were transformed into unregulated, removed and lumped highly opaque and often toxic investment instruments or funds with no relationships between borrowers and lenders. The amount of money in mortgage-driven or backed securities has grown to the tens of trillions of dollars, in fact larger than the world's gross product. This had become an unregulated, uncontrollable financial wilderness, driven solely by greed with each party transferring the hot risks of their toxic or risky mortgage backed securities (instruments or funds) to another level of greedy investors.

Brokers and banks exploited federal and state regulatory loopholes. These new types of high risk off-balance sheet investment instruments were created which required no money kept in reserve. In other words, they established a means of making money with having to put up no capital in reserve; in a way this became a hollow pyramid scheme in reverse.

These instruments, part of the global derivatives market which is estimated to be worth nearly $500 trillion or 10 times the global gross product have distorted the capital markets and introduced means for connecting markets all over the world, often with little understanding of the lack of backup, value of collateral, and the huge risks involved. It is amazing that many of the world's most respected financial institutions got sucked into this whirlpool of fraud and deception and down and forced their assets down the drain.

There is usually no real market price for many of these derivatives. Furthermore, the risks and consequently the values of these securities are impossible to assign as much of them are acquired with borrowed money. Considering the mortgage-backed security morass, the pyramid schemes were usually built by

- Lending money to non-creditworthy homeowners or housing speculators on the assumption that house values will go up and therefore the foreclosure price of the house will cover any outstanding balances of the loan or more, and furthermore the mortgage could anyway be sold to an investment bank for bundling with many other mortgages into a "Collateralized Debt Obligation" (CDO) which in turn is sold to other banks for additional bundling with other CDOs, sometimes bundled by risk category.
- Another risky derivative is the "Credit Default Swap" or CDS. Here an investor (bank, hedge fund, etc.) will undertake to cover any losses from non-payment of a loan against a quarterly payment under the CDS terms. Today more than $60 trillion in CDS are outstanding. These expose us to another financial crisis, now when an increasing number of debtors or borrowers may default on their loans.
- There is also something called "Structure Investment Vehicle" (SIV) which is designed to let investment banks involve hedge funds and investors get a high return without requiring the banks to maintain large reserves as security.

Altogether we were faced with an avalanche of ill-conceived and large fraudulent pyramid schemes or arrangements with the public or taxpayer taking all the risks with all the rewards received by unscrupulous lenders.

We now face a similar disaster in the student loan arena where unscrupulous lenders and for profit colleges collude to make huge profits while the public and taxpayers take all the risks. All this again under the guise of public interests such as home ownership for all now repeated under the slogan of college for all if needed, beneficial or affordable or not.

Appendix B: How Would the World and We Know How Great, Smart, Rich, and Good We are if We Would Not Tell Them?

Increasingly Americans delude themselves by self-praise instead of accomplishments. There are few broadcasts that do not start with that are we the best, the greatest, the richest, and the smartest. Few if any of these assertions have been proven or can be substantiated and even fewer achieve what they intend, which is make Americans feel more proud, richer, smarter or even more just, which is normally the intent or purpose of these exaggerations. They are supposed to raise or maintain the spirits, confidence, and trust of people yet are in many cases, outright insulting and well below the level and content of advertising used in much of the world at large.

Some commercials are outright ridiculous or misleading and advertisers should be sued for example as drug ads listing as side effects for users such as heart attacks, suicide, and other life threatening results, and the recommendation that if any of these occur users are advised to call their doctor right away. Not only is the ad misleading and dishonest, but it is outright ridiculous to suggest to call a doctor if a patient suffers a heart attack or commits suicide as a result of use of the medicine

America is the only Western or probably world country which permits the marketing of prescription drugs directly to patients. Anyway, it would be rather counterincentive and unfair for patients to recommend or even suggest to their doctor what drug to use. Doctors are supposed to know what to prescribe and not be influenced by patient requests or even suggestions.

In a way, American commercials as well as many newscasters engage in undiluted brainwashing which we discredited violently when done by the communists and others. It is just that our brainwashing deals more with personal and performance not political issues.

Appendix C: Employees of the U.S. Government (2007)

Departments

Department of Agriculture	120,000
Department of Commerce	29,780
Department of Defense (excluding Armed Forces)	821,911
Department of Education	6,100
Department of Energy	20,662
Department of Health and Human Services	140,900
Department of Housing and Urban Development	16,000
Department of the Interior	57,845
Department of Justice	58,396
Department of Labor	23,454
Department of State	23,738
Department of Transportation	74,855
Department of the Treasury	116,535
Total	1,610,176

Agencies

Action	1,976
CAB	743
Committee on Civil Rights	285
Commodity Futures Trading Commission	550
Consumer Product Safety Commission	880
Environmental Protection Agency	11,015
Equal Employment Opportunity Commission	3,779

Export-Import Bank	416
Federal Communications Commission	2,261
Federal Deposit Insurance Corporation	3,691
Federal Election Commission	227
Federal Emergency Management Agency	2,507
Subtotal	28,380
Federal Home Loan Bank Board	1,480
Federal Labor Relations Authority	362
Federal Maritime Commission	361
MCS	518
Federal Reserve	1,488
Federal Trade Commission	1,665
General Services Administration	37,835
ICA	8,675
International Commerce Commission	2,024
Merit System Board	503
National Aeronautics and Space Administration	22,613
National Credit Union	752
National Foundation of Arts	515
National Labor Relations Board	2,850
National Science Foundation	1,274
National Transportation Safety Board	388
Nuclear Regulatory Commission	2,851
Occupational Safety and Health Review Commission	183
Office of Personnel Management	6,728
Panama Canal Commission	8,410
Pension Benefit Guaranty Corporation	480
U.S. Postal Service	750,000
Railroad Retirement Board	1,895

Security and Exchange Commission	2,109
Small Business Administration	4,747
Tennessee Valley Authority	17,674
Arms Control	199
IDCA	6,310
Subtotal	913,269

Others

ITC	438
Veterans Administration	230,538

Total Federal Government Agencies — 1,144,245

Executive Branch

Executive Office of the President	1,897
Central Intelligence Agency	? estimated
Other	1,382
	3,279 + (28,000)

Judicial Branch — 14,117

Congress and Senate — 38,133

Others

Government Accountability Office	5,442
Government Printing Office	7,522
Library of Congress	5,049

Total Federal Government
(excluding Armed Forces and CIA) — **2,867,087**

INDEX

2008 Presidential election
  and election of the first black
    President 2, 121
  candidates of 10, 111
A123 Systems 112
advertising
  honesty in 92, 93
Afghanistan
  drug trade 21, 46
  war in 1, 6, 81, 101, 113, 129
African American
  and preventative medicine 93
agriculture
  America's performance 69, 70
  America's policy 68, 79
AIG
  bailout 13, 20, 81, 99
ambulance chasing 40, 41, 49, 50, 72, 116, 131
Amtrak 119
Anwar reserve 103, 108, 120
arbitration
  in malpractice suits 41, 50, 52, 73, 117, 143
automakers
  foreign production in US 99
  US bailout of 83, 99, 100
automobile
  US production 87
bailout
  argument against 100, 127
  of AIG. *See* AIG
  of financial services 12, 14, 19, 20, 26, 83, 99, 127, 148
  of Long Term Capital Management, 1998 20
  of mortgage lenders 80
  of US automakers 83, 99, 100

Bear Stearns
  bailout of 19, 81
bio-fuel 18, 69, 70, 106, 112
bonuses. *See* financial services
BP oil spill 54, 56, 58, 59, 60, 61
Brazil
  agriculture in 70
  economic growth 124
Bush, George W.
  plan to reduce greenhouse gas 105
  stimulus response 98
carbon tax 109, 110
  cap and trade 109
  carbon credits 109
  on imports 110
carbon trading 108, 109, 110
CEO
  compensation 13, 17, 19, 28, 29, 30, 33, 71, 100, 121
China 82
  CO_2 emissions 108, 109, 110
  decline in birth rate 10
  drug use in 47
  economic growth 87, 124
  education 63, 139
  employee training 94
  foreign debt to 14, 15, 91, 112
  government 146
  immigration 38, 141
  influence in Middle East 6
  infrastructure 53, 120
  trade 83, 84, 98, 130
Christianity 6, 124
Chrysler
  bailout 99, 100
class action suit 41, 43, 72, 74, 86, 93, 131, 133, 144
college. *See* education

Communism 6
Confucianism 124
Constitution 20, 95
consumerism 4, 21, 22, 23, 113, 125
consumption tax 49, 95, 113, 129, 145
continuous education 141, 142
  retraining 115
corruption 12, 13, 15, 16, 34, 35, 75, 76, 83, 95, 99, 123, 130, 132
Countrywide 71, 131
credit card debt 24, 25, 98
Credit Default Swaps (CDS) 14, 26
crime 21, 75, 143
  drug-related 45, 47
debt 15, 24
  credit card debt. *See* credit card debt
  foreign 14, 15, 24, 48, 61, 65, 79, 80, 82, 84, 91, 98, 129, 143, 148, 149
  mortgage 25, 26
  private equity financing 96
  public 65, 79, 85, 91, 98, 127, 146
  student loans. *See* student loans
default
  mortgages 26, 27
  student loans 140
Department of Defense 71
Department of Homeland Security 71
derivatives 13, 18, 81, 94, 97
discrimination
  immigrants 2
  in education 137, 138
disease
  prevention 45
  treatment 21, 45
doctors 41, 42, 44, 50, 72, 92, 116, 131, 132, 139
Dodd, Christopher 80
drugs 47
  illegal 20, 21, 45, 46, 47, 72, 76, 113
  laws 45, 46, 47, 143
  marketing 42, 43, 51, 92
  prescription 92
  prescriptions 47, 51, 72
  research 39

economic crisis of 2008 83, 99
economic stimulant 98
economy 1, 2, 4, 5, 9, 12, 14, 15, 20, 22, 24, 25, 27, 28, 31, 32, 33, 34, 37, 38, 39, 47, 53, 55, 56, 61, 62, 63, 68, 69, 70, 73, 76, 79, 80, 81, 82, 83, 84, 85, 86, 87, 89, 90, 91, 97, 98, 99, 102, 103, 107, 108, 112, 113, 118, 121, 123, 127, 130, 132, 133, 138, 140, 146, 147, 149, 150
  based on consumption 15, 22, 23, 48, 49, 80, 84, 91, 98, 107, 113, 124, 130, 149
education 1, 3, 4, 5, 37, 38, 42, 44, 48, 61, 62, 63, 64, 65, 66, 67, 68, 85, 94, 101, 113, 114, 115, 116, 123, 124, 132, 133, 135, 136, 137, 138, 139, 141, 142, 145, 146, 147, 149
  charter schools 137
  community colleges 64, 140
  for-profit colleges 64, 66, 136, 140
  No Child Left Behind 138
Education 61, 66, 67, 132, 136, 138, 139, 140
Eisenhower, Dwight 52
energy 3, 4, 5, 9, 10, 22, 83, 84, 85, 86, 102, 103, 104, 105, 106, 107, 109, 110, 111, 112, 113, 124
Enron 76
ethanol 3, 68, 102, 112
Ethanol 102, 106
EU 87, 109, 110
Europe 1, 9, 10, 28, 32, 38, 48, 53, 58, 80, 96, 100, 106, 107, 110, 119, 122, 124, 129, 130, 138, 145
European 1, 13, 14, 26, 30, 36, 91, 95, 96, 100, 104, 110, 120, 121, 122, 123, 128, 133, 139, 145
exports 15, 22, 27, 69, 70, 80, 90, 91, 110, 129, 142
Fannie Mae 80, 81
farming 68, 69, 70, 79, 80
  Farm Aid 68
  Farm Bill 68
  policies 68

subsidies 68, 90, 96
Federal Housing Administration 27
Federal Reserve 20, 27
financial aid 66
financial crisis 67
financial service 29, 31, 81, 94, 121, 131
financial services 83, 99
  and bonuses 13, 17, 28, 29, 33, 44, 74, 75, 81, 83, 100, 114, 148
  corporate oversight 83, 99
  golden parachute 13, 17, 29
Financial Times 11, 30
fine print 92
food 1, 3, 4, 5, 9, 10, 11, 15, 18, 21, 22, 23, 35, 43, 49, 51, 68, 69, 70, 79, 80, 84, 90, 98, 102, 106
foreclosures 12, 27, 28, 98
foreign exchange reserves 82
foreign imports 84
foreign trade 83
for-profit colleges 64
Frank, Barney 27, 80
Freddie Mac. *See* Fannie Mae
fuel efficiency 83
fuel surcharge 107
Galveston 10
gas 3, 18, 53, 55, 86, 103, 104, 105, 112, 119, 120
gasoline 18, 70, 95, 102, 105, 106, 119, 129, 144, 145
gasoline taxes 95
Gates, Robert 88
GDP 21, 22, 24, 27, 47, 62, 69, 82, 84, 85, 91, 113, 114, 129, 132, 142, 143
geothermal 104, 106, 107, 111
GI bill 66
global economic downturn of 2008 15
globalization 4, 11, 14
GM
  bailout 99, 100
Gore, Al 111
government 2, 3, 5, 12, 13, 14, 15, 16, 17, 18, 19, 20, 23, 26, 30, 34, 35, 36, 39, 42, 49, 53, 54, 56, 58, 59, 60, 61, 62, 64, 65, 67, 69, 71, 72, 74, 76, 79, 80, 81, 83, 84, 85, 86, 88, 89, 90, 91, 95, 96, 97, 98, 99, 100, 101, 107, 121, 127, 129, 130, 135, 136, 138, 139, 141, 142, 145, 146, 148, 150
Government 88, 90
greed 12, 13, 16, 17, 18, 33, 61, 100, 123, 127, 128, 130, 147, 148, 149
Greek debt crisis 91
greenhouse effects 109
gross product 87
Guerrera, Francesco 30
Gulf of Mexico 107, 108
Haiti earthquake 56
health care 1, 3, 4, 21, 35, 39, 40, 41, 42, 43, 44, 45, 47, 48, 50, 51, 52, 65, 85, 89, 90, 101, 113, 114, 115, 116, 118, 123, 132, 133, 135, 136, 140, 143, 146, 149
Health care 132
high school 62, 63, 64, 65, 67, 68, 101, 114, 115, 133, 137, 139, 140, 142
high speed rail 119, 120
highways 52, 94, 119
hospital 42, 43, 45
hospitals 39, 40, 41, 42, 43, 44, 50, 51, 52, 94, 101
housing crisis 79, 80, 85
housing slump 86
huge credit crisis of America in 2008 25
Hurricane Ike 18
Hurricane Katrina 10, 53, 54, 56, 58, 61
illegal immigration 39
immigrant 1, 2, 9, 10, 20, 36, 37, 38, 39, 130, 137
immigrants 120, 123, 128, 130, 148
immigration 36, 39, 121, 128
imports 2, 22, 23, 65, 70, 79, 80, 83, 85, 86, 91, 102, 104, 107, 108, 110, 112
incarceration 45

income 85, 91, 95, 96
income taxes 129, 144, 145
India 9, 10, 11, 32, 38, 109, 110, 124, 141
Indonesia 106
infant mortality 44
inflation xxxvii, 33, 34
influence peddling 148
infrastructure 1, 3, 7, 11, 18, 32, 33, 52, 53, 54, 55, 56, 75, 84, 90, 94, 107, 114, 118, 119, 120, 128, 130, 146
Infrastructure 52, 118, 128
insurance 14, 19, 26, 40, 43, 50, 68, 83, 92, 99, 116, 132, 141, 143
Interest payable 129
interest rates 97
international exchange rates 129
international trade 86, 110
interstate highway 54
Iraq
  war in 1, 3, 6, 81, 85, 101, 113, 129
Islam 124
Israel 41, 89, 90, 134, 143
Italy 37
Ivy League 141
jail 71, 130, 131
Jamaica 59
Japan 10, 28, 32, 48, 53, 63, 82, 83, 87, 94, 100, 107, 114, 119, 120, 121, 129, 138, 139, 141
Japanese 29, 30, 31
Jihadists 6
Jones Act 104
J. P. Morgan 19
Junk mail 57, 58
Justice Department 71
Kennedy, John 56
kickback 81
Korea 9, 10, 33, 53, 100, 119, 139, 141
Korean 29, 31, 33
Kyoto Protocol 108, 109, 110
Latin 2, 121, 128
Latinos 120
law 1, 16, 34, 40, 41, 47, 48, 50, 59, 71, 72, 73, 74, 75, 76, 77, 85, 88, 89, 92, 101, 113, 114, 131, 133, 141, 143, 144, 145, 149
law enforcement 1, 34, 47, 48, 71, 73, 74, 85, 89, 101, 113, 114, 131, 133, 143, 144, 145, 149
Law enforcement 133
lawyers 35, 40, 49, 50, 51, 52, 72, 73, 74, 75, 86, 96, 116, 131, 133, 139, 143, 144
legal system 42, 71, 74, 76, 117, 131
Lehman Brothers 13
leverage 96
liabilities 82, 96
liberal arts 62, 63, 65, 114, 115, 133, 136, 139
life expectancy 43, 51, 113, 115, 118
litigious 129
lobbying 35, 73, 74, 77, 135, 146, 150
Lobbying 76, 77
lobbyists 76, 77, 135, 148
Luxury assets 34
Madoff, Bernie 34, 76
Makis, John 97
malpractice 40, 41, 43, 44, 49, 50, 52, 74, 75, 116, 117, 143, 144
Malpractice 72, 132, 143
malpractice claims 116
malpractice insurers 116
management 83, 88, 97, 98, 99, 100, 103, 105
manufacturing 1, 11, 15, 29, 30, 31, 33, 38, 63, 64, 65, 79, 80, 83, 84, 87, 89, 99, 100, 102, 119, 124, 128, 129, 140, 141, 142, 146, 148
Marcelly, Angelo 71
market collapse of 2008 12
marketing 92, 93, 100
Medicaid 90
medical services 93
Medicare 90, 91
Merrill Lynch 19
Mexican 2
Mexico 39, 58

middle class 1, 2, 26, 30, 35, 46, 145, 148, 149
Middle East 6, 9, 58
Middle Eastern 7
Migrants 37
military 6, 9, 48, 50, 54, 84, 88, 90, 101, 113, 122, 123, 125, 128, 129
mining 87, 102, 103
Mitsui 33
Mortgage 16, 25
mortgage backed securities 26
Mumbai
  Attacks on 9
National Science Foundation 60
national security 6
Native American 130
New Deal 12
New Orleans 53, 56, 75
New York 79, 83, 94
New York Stock Exchange 94
Northeast Corridor 119
nuclear 104, 110, 118, 125
nuclear reactors 110
nurses 50, 64, 116, 133
Obama, Barack 7
  health care bill 50, 52
obesity 48, 51
Ocean Environmental Management 60
oil 86, 96, 102, 103, 104, 105, 107, 108, 111
outsourced 79, 86
outsourcing 64, 65, 96, 110, 129, 140
passenger rail 119, 120
Paulson, Henry
  bailout of financial services 127
petroleum 83, 102, 104, 105
petty criminals 71, 72, 76
pharmaceutical 51, 74
pharmaceuticals 79
Philippines 9
pollution 22, 56, 103, 109, 111, 118, 119
pork 90
poverty 1, 99, 130, 137, 138

predatory 16, 24, 25, 26
prescription 42, 51
President 12, 52, 59, 68, 85, 105
prestige assets 34
prestige sports 116, 137
prison 17, 21, 75, 101, 134, 143
prisoners 45, 133, 134, 143
private equity 83, 94, 96, 97, 99
Private equity 96, 97
productivity 15, 16, 21, 23, 31, 44, 53, 55, 63, 68, 89, 90, 96, 122, 123, 125, 129, 142, 150
professors 33, 142
Prudential 19
public accountants 96
Puerto Rico 9
Reaganism 14
recession 12, 25, 80, 81, 83
reeducation 142
refugees 37
regulation 4, 12, 14, 15, 18, 19, 27, 28, 34, 39, 44, 61, 92, 97, 110, 114, 123, 124, 147
regulations 113
Representatives 148
Republican 95
research universities 66, 136, 141
retirement age 63, 115
retraining 94, 116, 138, 142, 147
Roabini, Nouriel 79
Rome 10
Roosevelt 68
Roosevelt, Franklin 12
Russia 1, 6, 11, 56
Saudi Arabia 61
saving 4, 58, 71
savings 12
school budget 116
school systems 62, 116, 137
science 11, 29, 36, 48, 62, 67, 88, 92, 113, 123, 124, 128, 135, 136, 141
SEC 13, 34
securitization 81, 85, 94
Senators 148
September 2008 meltdown 18

shipping and handling 92
Shopping 23
Singapore 29, 46, 140
social entitlements 145
socialism 12, 14, 95
Social Security 61, 63, 64, 65, 91, 113, 114, 115, 140, 142
South American 14
sovereign wealth funds 82
Soviet Union 6, 118
S&P 500 30
Spain 9, 37, 103, 120
Spanish 2, 120, 128
special interests 5, 76, 113, 121, 135
sports 33, 52
Stewart, Martha 71, 131
Strategic Petroleum Reserves 103, 104
student loans 63, 64, 65, 66, 67, 114, 140
student-teacher ratio 65
sub-prime 79, 98, 99
sub-prime financial systems 79
sub-prime housing 79
sub-prime mortgage 3, 12, 15, 17, 19, 24, 26, 61, 71, 85, 94, 131
sub-prime mortgages 17, 26
Suffolk University 33
Supreme Court 77
Taiwan 10, 141
tar sands 108
tax 85, 90, 91, 95, 96, 102, 105, 107
tax code 96
tax collectors 90
tax cuts 148
taxes 90, 91, 95, 105, 107, 111, 114, 136, 145, 146, 148
tax evasion 96
tax exemptions 96
tax rates 113, 129
tax shortfall 90
teachers 62, 65, 116, 132, 138, 139, 142
technology 11, 32, 36, 41, 44, 45, 48, 51, 52, 53, 54, 58, 65, 69, 84, 87, 89, 90, 93, 94, 104, 106, 107, 108, 111, 113, 116, 118, 119, 123, 124, 129, 135, 141, 142, 146, 148
Technology 42, 141
terrorism 1, 7
Terrorism 9
terrorists 6, 9
tobacco 46
too big to fail 99
top earners 85
tort reform 143
trade 3, 4, 14, 15, 18, 21, 22, 29, 39, 61, 64, 81, 83, 87, 88, 96, 105, 107, 109, 125, 129, 134, 140, 141, 142, 148
  deficit 14, 23, 79, 98, 107, 142
trade imbalance 87
trade schools 134, 140
trains 19, 53
transportation 4, 58
tuition 64, 141
UK 37, 63, 95, 114
UN 109, 110
unemployment 98, 99
UNEP 106
UN Food and Agricultural Organization Price Index 69
U.N. Food and Agriculture Organization 18
union 83, 99
unions 89
universities 38, 60, 61, 64, 66, 118, 133, 134, 136, 141
U.S. Government 14, 15
US Postal Service
  deficit 24, 58
  junk mail 24, 57, 58
Value Added Tax 49, 91, 95, 145
venture capital 94, 97
Vietnam 9, 32
Wall Street 12, 18, 19, 49
Washington 76, 77, 83, 84, 99, 111, 119, 135, 148
weak dollar 80, 103
wealth class 35
wellness care 43
wind power 103, 110

172

Woods Hole Oceanographic Institute 60
World Bank 38, 109
 Carbon Finance Unit 109
World Export of Goods and Services 87
World War I 125
World War II 6, 9, 54, 56, 87, 118, 125
WTO 88, 110